Messages of Ascended Masters

D1373198

Words of Wisdom
10

Dictated to the Messenger
Tatyana N. Mickushina

June – July 2009

Tatyana N. Mickushina

Words of Wisdom - 10

Dictated to the Messenger
Tatyana N. Mickushina

This book contains the messages received by Tatyana N. Mickushina from the Ascended Masters. Up to now 20 books have been written and published in the Russian language.

The messages are constantly being translated into different languages by people all around the world. At present there are 19 languages that the messages are being translated into.

This particular book consists of the messages received during the summer cycle in the year 2009 (from June 20 to July 10, 2009). It also includes two messages received earlier (April 22 and May 24, 2009) and the messages published previously that are related to the subject of this book.

Websites:
http://sirius-eng.net (English version)
http://sirius-ru.net (Russian version)

ISBN: 1-4505-4044-9
ISBN-13: 9781450540445

Table of Contents

3

From the author

I was born and I live in Russia in the south of western Siberia in the city of Omsk. During all my life I have been praying and asking God to grant me an opportunity to work for Him.

In 2004 I was granted a Messenger's Mantle of the Great White Brotherhood and received an opportunity to bring the Words of the Masters to people. During the years 2005-2010 at certain periods of time I have been receiving messages of the Ascended Masters in a special way.

I am very happy that with the help of many people the messages I received have been translated into English and the English-speaking readers can become familiar with them.

The only thing the Ascended Masters want is to spread their Teaching throughout the world. The Masters give their messages with the feeling of great Love.

Love has no limits. There are no boundaries between the hearts of people living in different countries, there are no boundaries between the worlds. The boundaries exist only in the consciousness of people.

The Masters appeal through me to every human living on planet Earth.

From Siberia with Love,

Tatyana Mickushina

Preface

This book contains the Messages of the Masters of Wisdom, or the Ascended Masters, or the Masters of Shambala, or the Great White Brotherhood, or the Teachers of humanity, or the Hierarchy of the Forces of Light. People call them by different names. These beings have reached the next evolutionary step in their development.

The information contained in the Messages belongs neither to any particular system of beliefs nor to any concrete religion.

The substance of these Messages is that humanity is going through a very important stage of its development when it should give up focusing on the self, on the ego. It is necessary to transit to the new level of consciousness where man understands that he is not a mere physical body. At that level of consciousness man realises his Divine timeless nature, feels his interconnection with every living creature, with the entire universe. There arises a feeling of infinite Love, Compassion and Mercy towards everything that exists in space. At that level of consciousness such negative phenomena as hatred, wars, jealousy, vengeance, violence, ignorance, and fear are impossible.

And if in the near future humanity does not straighten its course in accordance with the stream of evolution, the most drastic consequences of its wrong collective choice are possible, even to the extent of a global cataclysm.

The Messages of the Masters of Wisdom contain concrete recommendations on how humans should act in order to change their consciousness.

These Messages are a helping hand extended through the worlds.

This book contains the Messages that the Ascended Masters were giving during the summer cycle of dictations from June 20th to July 10th, 2009.

The previous nine cycles of dictations were published in the books *Words of Wisdom*, *Words of Wisdom 2*, *Words of Wisdom 3*, *Words of Wisdom 4*, *Words of Wisdom 5*, *Words of Wisdom 6*, *Words of Wisdom 7*, *Words of Wisdom 8*, and *Words of Wisdom 9*.

The dictations are located in the book according to their chronological order.

The Appendix contains dictations from April 22nd and May 24th, 2009, which have not previously been published, and also dictations which were published previously and which are related to the subject of the dictations of the summer cycle 2009.

Editorial note

Stop evading the tasks of evolution

Sanat Kumara, June 20, 2009

I AM Sanat Kumara, having come to you again today. I am happy that I have an opportunity to give messages to the Earth's humanity. We are not always afforded such an opportunity, as the situation on the Earth changes and the consciousness of individuals is subject to changes to a great extent.

I have come today in order to give you an idea of what is happening on the planet. Many of you, watching the situation around you in the physical plane, think of what is going on. Everything seems to be as usual, but still has somehow subtly altered. Moreover, it seems to many of you that the whole world has gone mad. And this will not be far from the truth.

Really, we laid our account with a bigger transformation of the consciousness of people. We reckoned on an opportunity for a greater co-operation when we started to work through our messenger in Russia. And now we are watching with surprise the repetition of the sad experience of America. The Russian people have taken the same tack. They wonder at the messages, look upon them as at an oddity, and our messages and our Teaching only occupy their consciousness for as long as the time necessary for the reading of a dictation.

Unfortunately, we have not yet got what we expected. We do not see readiness for co-operation. We do not see those individuals who are to such extent permeated with our Teaching that they are ready to sacrifice everything they have, to sacrifice their very life in order for their unselfish service for the good of the evolutions of planet Earth to turn the consciousness of many people living on the planet in the direction of knowing the Divine Truth.

We have realised that our hopes have again fallen short of our expectations. We have again encountered the lethargy of human consciousness and its unpredictability. Well, we have drawn our lessons and are ready to continue the movement on the path of evolutionary development. For you hope remains, but in order for that hope to come true you should think hard about whether you do everything the way you should do.

Since the situation on the planet is heating up we do not have any more time to speak too much and for a long time. We draw on the Teaching which has been given already. And in order for you to continue moving you should devote every day of your life to the change of your consciousness. I understand very well and am aware of the fact that you are immersed in the illusion and the illusion is increasing more and more with each day.

Do understand us as well. We are concerned and care about the salvation of each soul who is still asleep but hears our call, our exhorting and our Teaching in his or her doze. You still cannot distinguish whether what you hear from us is a continuation of your dream or already the sounds of a New Day.

However, we are satisfied with a little: you hear us and this already gladdens us.

Never stop aspiring. Never allow the illusion to capture your consciousness completely.

I do not lose hope, and I assure all the cosmic councils that the humanity of planet Earth is able to progress on the evolutionary path of development.

However, there is less and less time left. I will not disclose the terms which are being discussed and the dates of the impending events. What good will this do to you?

Those who have been sleeping – for them there will be no significance in what is going to happen. Those who are awakened – no harm will come to them.

Only those few are remaining who hear my words as if in a doze and forget about them immediately after reading my message.

But even to you I will not disclose the terms either, because the time does not matter at all if you don't manage to master the transformation of your consciousness now.

I have come to remind you that now very much, if not to say everything, depends on each of you who is in embodiment.

Stop evading the tasks of evolution, stop hiding in your safe nooks and continuing secretly to play your childish games. You have already grown out of all the possible limits when it was necessary for you to master our Teaching.

Now I have to tell you with full responsibility that the whole world and its destiny depend on those few who have come into embodiment exactly in this time with a definite mission and goal but who have been carried away with games in the illusion to such an extent that they have missed all the given deadlines. And we are facing the need to either extend the terms or make you awaken from your lethargy by force.

Every time we talk and warn, and every time your consciousness refuses to believe that everything is very serious. Let this message of mine make you open your eyes at least for a while and see the danger that is threatening mankind if it is not able, in the face of those few who have come into embodiment exactly for this purpose, to do what the Cosmic Law requires to be done now. And now it is required to prove that mankind is capable of cooperation with the Higher Worlds, that mankind can and wants to develop and follow the ascending path of evolutionary development.

I am telling you all this openly and earnestly, because I have taken upon myself a responsibility for mankind of earth. And I will continue waking you up and forcing you to awaken until you do this.

You cannot imagine how difficult it is for me to convince the Great Central Sun that mankind needs a little more time and a little more energy. It is a pity that you cannot appreciate and understand the care and guardianship that your senior brothers and sisters, the Ascended Masters, are rendering to you now.

I will be silent now, because everything that I have told requires time for thinking it over. Do promise me that you will reread this message of mine at least three times in different states of your consciousness.

I have come to you today in order to make one more attempt to evoke a response from your hearts.

I AM Sanat Kumara. Om.

We cannot lose a single minute now

Lord Surya, June 21, 2009

I AM Surya.

I have come today for an important talk, and I hope that our conversation today will induce your souls to those actions and steps that are necessary at this stage.

Now I would like to remind you of some things that we have discussed already in our previous messages[1], but about which it bears repeating. The speech is about the attitude you have towards us, the Ascended Hosts, and the attitude you have to our messages.

Nowadays many people have imagined that they can receive our messages. And very many of them receive messages in truth and try to publish them as widely as possible.

Well, this is your right. God cannot deprive you of your free will and forbid you from acting on it. However, we can give a Teaching on the karmic responsibility for the misqualification of the Divine energy.

Every time you strive to get in contact with, as it seems to you, the Higher world, you should slow down a little and analyse the state of your consciousness, since the state of your consciousness imprints everything you do. You should also analyse your motive, as your motive determines the vector of your action.

Both of those are very important. Every action you perform in the physical plane or in more subtle planes

---

[1] Lord Surya is talking about the dictations containing the Teaching on making distinctions. Some of the dictations and excerpts from the dictations on this topic are published in the book "Ascension" and are also available in English on the Sirius website: **www.sirius-eng.net**

of thoughts and feelings is coloured by you and serves the manifestation of either the forces multiplying the illusion or the forces contributing to contracting the illusion.

That is why the side of the forces on which you act depends on what kind of aspirations you have.

For example, you are driven by mere curiosity, and you decide to play at receiving messages from the subtle plane. There is nothing bad in this. You can experiment. But you must know and observe the safety rules when communicating with the subtle world.

You do not sit at the wheel of a modern jetliner without having passed through a course of proper training and without the guidance of an experienced instructor. Why do you think that when you enter into communication with the subtle world you can do so without having undergone the training and without ascertaining that the initiative you undertake is safe?

Many of you, very many think for some reason that they can practise receiving messages from the subtle plane. And you do it, notwithstanding the many and frequent warnings which we give. And I would not spend the precious Divine opportunity on giving another message on this topic, if not for those many and very frequent cases when people strive to receive messages and to get in contact with the subtle world, do this and, as it seems to them, succeed in this, but then a moment comes when they can no longer return to the initial point. They go too far in their experiments. The invisible world, the astral world with its tenants captures an inexperienced soul and starts controlling and manipulating it. And you turn from an experimentalist into a laboratory rat for the beings of the astral plane, who completely seize the power over your lifestream, and you no longer belong to yourself, you have to obey constant orders and commands of the beings which act through you and manipulate you.

You may and must experiment. But why not start with safer exercises on changing your consciousness and on purifying your consciousness? And why as a first step won't you start experimenting in the sphere of distinguishing what in the reality around you corresponds to the Divine patterns and what, on the contrary, is a manifestation of the negative, non-divine forces?

Each of you sooner or later in your life faces such circumstances which start stirring you up and raise a storm of emotions in you. You encounter manifestations which make you suffer, become nervous and act in order to secure yourselves and to return to the comfort zone. Isn't it true that many of you are constantly experiencing anxiety, fear, aggression or depression? Why do you experience these negative states of consciousness? One of the reasons you have these states of consciousness lies in the fact that you have consciously or unconsciously subordinated yourselves to the astral plane. And it did not even occur to you when you were engaged in your experiments on receiving messages. You subjected yourselves to the astral plane when you were consuming alcohol, nicotine, eating meat, watching horror films, blood-and-guts thrillers, porno films. By all this you tied yourselves to the astral plane, and now you have to obey its influence and reap the fruits of your actions.

You will say that the majority of people living on earth do the things I have enumerated. Yes, this is true, and the majority of people living on earth are subject to the influence of the astral plane.

I come to you in order to direct the vector of your aspiration towards more subtle and higher worlds.

I strive to direct your attention towards the Divine patterns and manifestations of the Divine world. And believe me, when you start making a distinction you will be able to orient yourselves in the vibrations of non-manifested planes of existence. And the astral plane forces will no longer have you at their beck and call; you will be able to distinguish the vibrations of everything surrounding you at the manifested and non-manifested level and to give preference to the Divine patterns, declining of your free will the low-vibrational surrogates that lead your souls by the path of death and hell.

It seems to you that there is nothing terrible in some of your little weaknesses and in your indulgence to your low instincts and habits. I am telling you that now the time has come when you have to consciously make a decision and get rid of every non-divine manifestation inside you and, as a result, you will be able to get rid of the non-divine manifestations in your world because the matter obediently reflects your consciousness.

I would not give so much attention to these simple instructions if I saw that the instructions of the Ascended Hosts were being executed by you at least to a small degree. The majority of those who read our messages pay no heed to the information and the keys to the safe development of humanity which we give and this information does not bring them to any actions, neither at the level of mind nor in the physical plane.

Do realise that the time is such now that not a single minute can be lost. You have no time to postpone this work on changing yourselves, changing your consciousness.

I have given you the necessary instructions. Don't expect a miracle to come from outside. If you are not ready inside of you, no miracle can help you. A huge amount of the Divine energy is spent on the preparation and manifestation of any miracle, and in order for a miracle to take place you should prove that you are ready for the transformation of your consciousness and do all the necessary things for this transformation.

And now I want to remind you of the dispensation of letters to the Karmic Board[2]. Right now in these days the sitting of the Karmic Board is taking place that can consider your requests and give you the help you are asking for. However, when making a decision on rendering help, the Karmic Board is always guided by the degree of purity of your motives and the sincerity of your search for change. It is impossible to deceive God, it is impossible to make God play by your human rules.

The time has come when you must understand that all the possible deadlines have passed.

I do not know what the general decision of the Great Central Sun will be, but still do not forget in your letters to ask for mercy for planet Earth since the state in which the planet is now needs the urgent involvement of the legions of Light. The balance has been disturbed and it has been disturbed not without the participation of each of you.

I AM Surya.

---

[2] The information about the dispensation of letters to the Karmic Board is published in the book "Words of Wisdom - 9" and is also available in English on the Sirius website: **www.sirius-eng.net**

I am calling you into the future!

Saint Archangel Michael, June 22, 2009

I AM Archangel Michael.

I have come surrounded by the angels of the blue flame. And today I would like you to fully concentrate your attention on the message that I am giving you.

Now and for the coming days, the time has come when we must focus our efforts on helping the planet. And this is my message and my warning to you.

I have been carefully choosing the words and thinking about how to get a simple truth over to you that you have reached such time when you have to share with the Ascended Hosts the responsibility for everything that happens on the planet.

You are not eager to take over this responsibility, yet to take the responsibility for the planet you will have to. And that is the next level of consciousness onto which you should rise.

You are still worried about what is happening around you, you are so enthralled by the illusion that surrounds you at home and at work, and which is shown on TV. However, there are much more important and substantial things that the time has come for you to start thinking about.

The entire world, the physical and the subtle planes of existence are trembling because of many of your actions, thoughts and feelings. Both I and the other beings of Light, sometimes watch with a shudder another burst of negative energy which humanity releases through its folly. Every time an uncontrolled release of negative energy happens, it takes a great effort by numerous beings of Light to balance out the

16

situation so that the consequences for the physical plane do not become catastrophic.

Now the time has come when you, the best representatives of the human community, must share with us, the Ascended Hosts, the responsibility for planet Earth, for everything that happens on the planet. And this is the level of consciousness which must be truly achieved by you in the nearest future.

Stop looking at the people that surround you, stop following the lead you see around you and on TV screens. The time is coming when you should follow the direction which you get from your hearts. There are more subtle energies and processes that are occurring around you on more subtle planes. And these processes are reflected within you as certain states of your consciousness. It is not always that the things occurring in the subtle planes can be consciously understood by you and not everything reaches your external consciousness, but there does exist a certain intuition, premonition and inspiration. And if you become honest with yourself, if you enter your heart and feel the vibrations of a more subtle plane, then you will undoubtedly hear the warning tocsin ringing on planet Earth. And this tocsin is a danger signal. It is an indicator of the ill-being of the planet.

How can the situation be changed and what can be done now in order for the preponderance of forces on the planet to open up an opportunity of a bright future again?

I think that it will not be superfluous to remind you that be the times ever so hard for you and be the thoughts and states filling you so heavily, you still must find the strength to say:

"I know that these states are not real. I know that the illusion is strong, but I am ready to oppose all the power of my Love pouring from my heart against the illusory forces. I love this world. I love God and His creation, and I will not allow this world to be destroyed. Beloved Archangel Michael and the angels of protection, I am asking you to use my lifestream to help the legions of Light. I know that nothing will happen to my planet as long as at least one lightbearer acts consciously on the side of the powers of Light."

As soon as we gather a sufficient number of individuals who are ready in their hearts to firmly support the Light, then we will be able to ask the Great Central Sun and all the Cosmic committees for mercy so that the Earth gets help and this help comes without delay.

Much is upon the die at this moment. Most human individuals are not ready for a change of consciousness. And volunteers are needed to demonstrate a new level of consciousness, the consciousness that is not tied to the physical or astral plane but is ready to cooperate with the Higher Worlds.

And when there is a sufficient number of individuals capable of demonstrating a new consciousness, then, due to their efforts, the consciousness of other people will begin to change too.

You all are interconnected in more subtle planes of being. And there is a necessity for a higher frequency of consciousness to resonate like a tuning fork in space, so that the souls of those people who are stuck in the illusion rise again and cast their glances heavenward.

I envy you, those who are incarnated at this very tough time. Because the future of the planet and of millions of souls who are caught in the illusion and do not see daylight depend on your ability to keep your consciousness pure, heavenward and accordant with the Higher Worlds.

Lead by example! Be brave, be enduring and be inventive. Invent the ways that will carry millions of people to a new level of consciousness. Do sound on the top note. Do set the pattern!

I am calling you into the future!

I AM Archangel Michael!

Your task is to learn to win in the higher plane

Serapis Bey, June 23, 2009

I AM Serapis Bey. Today I have come! With every passing day it is more and more difficult for us to evoke a response from your hearts. Mankind is inevitably heading for destruction. And yet we hope against hope, because exactly when the situation seems to be hopeless and there is no way out of the existing situation, exactly at this moment something comes that can be called a Divine miracle and the situation changes.

How often there were moments in the history of mankind when it seemed that there was just bottomless gloom ahead. But every time literally at the edge of doom self-sacrificing souls appeared in the very last moment who took responsibility upon themselves for the further march of the earthly evolution at those critical moments.

I know that among those who are reading my message now there are very many light souls. You came into embodiment many times at the most critical moments of the history of earth. And now your all-out effort and resources are required again.

You just need to take courage and raise your eyes above the illusion surrounding you.

Imagine that you are in a bad dream. The night will pass and the sun will shine again. And in broad daylight all your night fears and nightmares will seem unreal.

You are in a dream. You are in a deep dream of illusion.

Now the time has come when you need to gather all your strength and abilities and make a step forward.

You are knights. You are warriors. And many things depend on your effort now. But it does not mean you must take a sword and put on a suit of heavy armour in the physical plane. You must clothe yourselves in the armour of your spirit. And you must raise your sword of spirit - your sword of Kundalini – which is the only one able to separate the real from the unreal both within you and in the reality around you.

You are warriors, but your task is not to battle constantly in the physical plane. Your task is to learn to win in the higher plane – in the plane of your emotions and thoughts. Exactly when you achieve a victory over your thoughts, feelings and the negative states you experience, you will win in the physical plane of being - because your achievements in the higher planes will without doubt transform the physical plane.

You do not need to look for rows of warriors which you have to join, because in the higher plane you are a mighty army of Light. And you are invincible and invulnerable as long as you keep your consciousness at the Divine level.

All that is needed from you now is to clothe yourselves in the real Divine consciousness and not to give up the level of your consciousness throughout the day and day by day.

Imagine you are a paragon of perfection in the physical plane. At the cost of incredible effort and inner work you maintain your consciousness at the highest possible level. And it is quite hard to do while being in the imperfect manifestation. Yet when you manage to maintain the maximum level of consciousness, your vibrations rise so high that every imperfection that you meet in your world is forced to manifest itself. You are our warriors and you are torches highlighting for us the imperfection within the illusion. All that God wants is to have the wheat separated from the chaff in your world as quickly as possible. It is only when good grains are harvested and the weeds are made into a bonfire, will the time come when the Ascended Masters will be able to come to your world.

Therefore, never say die and never say that everything is bad. Everything is proceeding exactly according to the Divine plan. And each of you who will summon up courage to bear the burden of Light at this time - each of you will be ensured protection by the angelic hosts.

You are staring at the world around you in consternation and the situation seems hopeless to you. Do not get sad about the things that are not suitable for the further evolution. Have your feet firmly on the ground and make your calls to Heaven.

Your mission and your role at this difficult time are to bear the strain of the battle and to hold out in the battle.

Only the battle is taking place in the higher plane, in the layers of the dense astral plane closest to the physical plane. That is why you feel the battle. You go to bed and wake up with a strong feeling that you were in a fierce battle all night. And that is actually true. The best warriors of Light know no rest day or night, because you cannot lose any precious time as there is very little time left.

But then you will remember about your deeds of valour. The time in which you live now is unforgettable! No matter how hard it is for you, you need to realise that it is necessary to hold out and it is necessary to withstand. You cannot fall into despondency! Love the pressure, love the battle!

It is said that only the bravest and the most devoted will be able to continue the evolution.

I have been happy to give you this message today!

I AM Serapis Bey.

I have come to disabuse your souls of the darkness which has benighted planet Earth

Lord Shiva, June 24, 2009

I AM Shiva!

I have come to you again today. It was not worth coming in order to give you the Teaching, because you do not value our messages and our Teaching.

Every time we meet the reaction of humanity towards our efforts to come into contact and to offer cooperation we feel like dropping everything and starting from the beginning.

You are not ready and do not want to make efforts to become ready for collaboration.

The illusion still holds control over your beings.

And even when you try to get an insight into the subject of our Teaching, you still remain more under the influence of the illusion than under our influence which we are trying to exert on you through our messages.

You are not able to overcome that barrier which is invisibly present within yourselves. You do not want and do not wish to take a decisive step and to overcome the illusion, first of all in your consciousness. And that is why we are facing a choice: either to leave humanity, to leave it to its own devices, or yet to continue our efforts and exhortations.

Sometimes it seems to me that it is impossible to rouse humanity by dint of persuasion. However, if we were to give up our control, humanity would not be able to survive on its own even for one earth day. You are always in ward of the Higher Beings of this universe.

Your civilisation will be destroyed within 24 hours as soon as we stop putting energy into supporting your civilisation.

The whole point is that too much of an effort has been made already so that humanity starts taking steps in the direction of the evolution and making informed and fairly mature decisions.

Those few souls that are ready to follow our directions are isolated and feel like white crows in the surrounding world. And when I think about these few, when I enjoy the riches of their spiritual experience that they have been gathering like bees during the period of many earthly incarnations, I join the banners of the advocates of the continuation of the earthly experiment.

There is always a little gold, but even though there is rather more barren rock, people continue mining gold. And we will continue to give your aura an opportunity to gain a golden glow.

Amidst the noise, dirt and dust of your cities it is very hard to recognise those people who are enlightened by the Divine Light. You are looking for God where there is no God and where He cannot be. You are looking for God amongst the prosperity of the world. However, we come to teach you to make your distinction. God is ever present in your world, however you should observe. Within each of you God is present. You need to observe.

There are very quiet moments of goodness in your life when everything seems to die down. You hear the silence amidst the noise of the city. Everything falls into silence. And at such moments God quietly comes to you. He appears from the bottom of your being and extends His influence on everything around you. And if you were able to feel such moments of presence of the divine in your world more often, then, having tasted that goodness, you would forever turn away from those surrogates which your civilisation offers you. It is impossible to confuse the goodness God gives you with the surrogates you meet everywhere in your world.

I would wish that you manage to capture those states of inner silence and quietness in your world. And I would wish that you manage to keep the memory of these states even when everything around you is collapsing.

There are true states when you abide in God. And you must intend to remain in such states. This way the Divine world can pour into your manifested world from inside of you. And this way the imperfection of your world will gradually abate like fire that cannot find more fuel for itself.

Only you yourselves make it possible for the imperfection of your world to exist. Only you yourselves direct your energy to the imperfection and it continues to exist. Stop, wait, think of what you are doing. Stop running around in circles like a stupid donkey after a carrot from day to day, from embodiment to embodiment. Each of you has his own carrot. For some of you it is sexual pleasures, for others it is your career which you call self-realisation for some reason, for others it is different narcotic substances, gambling, and entertainment.

How many different things did humanity invent in order to obstruct the way to the only Truth – God, who resides in the peace of your hearts.

Enter the peace of your heart. And you will have the paragon with which to compare the things you meet in your lives. You will compare the states that arise within you when you come across the toys of your world and contrast them with this state of the Divine harmony and quietness.

You need to voluntarily give up all those masses of different things that are present in your world but are useless for you in the future world.

It is very simple to cut the Gordian knot of your civilisation with one blow of the trident. However, every grain of the best human achievements has to be protected and preserved. The best achievements of the human civilisation considerably exceed the achievements of other systems of worlds. But as a counter-weight there are so many things in your world that make the Higher Worlds shudder and that should be committed to the cosmic fire.

You are in the crucible of the cosmic furnace. And the process of separation of gold from waste rock is occurring within you. And the percentage of the gold souls who will transit to the Golden Age of humanity is exactly equal to the percentage of gold in the waste rock on the Earth.

I have come in order to disabuse your souls of the darkness which has benighted planet Earth.

I AM Shiva!

A Teaching on the choice and the Path

Lord Maitreya, June 25, 2009

I am Maitreya, having come to you.

Today I have come to think together with you and to hold discourse, spiritual discourse with you. I would like to appeal directly to your soul. I would like you to discard your thoughts and worries of the day at least for a while. Your states of consciousness during the day are such that they create an insuperable barrier between our worlds. How can I explain to you and how can I give you that state of consciousness which will enable you to understand me?

I have come with assurance that the time for a serious talk is ripe. And this talk is now necessary for those souls who had already been following the Path of the Ascended Masters, but at some part of that Path started to experience doubts and uncertainty.

You are overwhelmed and bewildered by the masses of information scattered around everywhere in your world. This information is about the many new ways through which you will miraculously transform yourselves and will become ready to live in the New World.

Remember the words of Jesus about the broad road that leads to hell and about the narrow gate that leads to the Kingdom of God.[3]

Your thrashing about and your effort to deceive the Divine Law and to take up a position inappropriate for you in the cosmic chain are wrong from the start and

---

[3] Enter through the narrow gate. For wide is the gate and broad is the road that leads to destruction, and many enter through it. But small is the gate and narrow the road that leads to life, and only a few find it. (Matthew 7:13-14)

27

necessitate immediate reformation. You cannot occupy the energy level that does not conform with your consciousness. All that you should care about is the level of your consciousness. And the purity of your consciousness can neither be attained with the help of other people, nor bought for money or obtained at a seminar. Only you yourselves with the help of your personal efforts are able to get free from those energies that prevent you from progressing on the path of evolution.

There are people among you who are convinced that they will manage to live through some transition and to continue their life of ease in the New World.

They suppose that they can perform the transition to the new level of evolution without giving up their old energies and habits. You cannot be operated on for alteration of your DNA or for removal of your karma. You yourselves must show your ability for the further evolution with your own achievements and your own efforts. And this ability is not measured by the number of books you have read, seminars you have attended or the number of rosaries you have read and meditations you have practised.

Your level of consciousness is determined by those Divine qualities which you acquire on your Path. It is impossible to play at Service, self-sacrifice, unselfishness or Love.

You must master these qualities, and they must become inherent in you. It is exactly acquiring these qualities that enables you to alter the very structure of your DNA, the informational code that will allow you to exist in the world to come.

There were beings in the history of this universe who tried to deceive the Law and to ascend to the level inappropriate for them with the help of witchcraft, black magic and different impure spiritual practices. And you know, none of those individuals managed to stay on the level inappropriate for them for any significant period of time.

You can jump from a skyscraper and believe you are flying for some time, but these will be just moments that will end in your hitting the ground.

In order to learn how to fly you must alter your inner state of consciousness. Do direct the energy you waste during the day on idle talk, entertainment and watching TV onto the work upon your qualities. Do not think that any of the most perfect techniques and spiritual practices will have an effect on you if you are unable to overcome the resistance of the unreal part within you, if you are unable to come out of the shell of the human consciousness.

You should get rid of your carnal mind, cast off your human consciousness, just as a snake sheds its skin. You need to obtain a new consciousness. You will not be able to continue your evolution without this. Without this your development as a species is not possible - as a man of reason who must become a Divine man.

I have come to you today in order to direct the vector of your aspirations from the pursuit of external ways of obtaining merits to the way you are taught by the Ascended Masters - the attainment of the inner merits. These are the riches that you cannot be deprived of; these are the riches that defy moth or rust.[4] These are the riches that are your treasures in Heaven.

---

[4] Do not store up for yourselves treasures on earth, where moth and rust destroy, and where thieves break in and steal. But store up for yourselves treasures in heaven, where moth and rust do not destroy, and where thieves do not break in and steal. For where your treasure is, there your heart will be also. (Matthew 6:19-21)

And you must learn to switch from your illusory reality to the reality that is the Divine world.

It is as hard for you to keep your human attachments and to concurrently transit to the spiritual world as sitting between two chairs at the same time or holding two large watermelons in one hand.

The time is ripe for you to make a choice. Which of the two worlds are you choosing: your illusory world or the real world of God? The future of humanity and the path it will follow in the immediate future depend on how the majority of humans will answer this question.

I have given a very clear Teaching on the choice and the Path.

All you need is to understand this Teaching.

I wish you success on your Path!

I AM Maitreya.

Why not everyone can follow the Path

Beloved Jesus, June 26, 2009

I AM Jesus.

I have come to you. You work tough in your world. You are constantly residing in the environment which is not dignified for man. You have got used to the sty smell. And now after a long wait the time is coming when a new consciousness must appear amidst all your chaos and hustle and bustle. The advent of this consciousness is unobservable, but the new consciousness must inevitably come to your world. And there are enough volunteers who have manifested a desire to pass my Path and to undergo a crucifixion in matter as a reward for their devotion and service.

Yes, in your world there is no reward and there cannot be any for your service and for the spiritual feat you are bearing which is similar to the cross that I was bearing to Calvary. And those of you who wish to earn fame, to come into prominence, to receive honours or get money and who are ready to do the necessary work for the Masters for the sake of getting all this – your hour has not come yet. You will not be able to pass my Path.

In order for you to be able to step onto the Path of Christ you need to make this decision within your hearts. And I will render my hands-off assistance and lend my support to each of you who wants to follow my Path sincerely within your heart. But you need to realise that there is no way back from this Path. You have to understand the entire responsibility for the fact that you are going on the Path of Christ. You cannot wish to follow the Path of Christ today and leave your cross in the attic and continue enjoying the pleasures of your world tomorrow.

You make the choice inside yourself. And you must weigh thoroughly how strong your aspiration is. Very many people decide to follow the Path in the first flush of enthusiasm and under the influence of their mood. But a day or two passes and their determination evaporates. New pleasures overtake their being and they forget about the decision they made. However, for you it means a big step back. Every time the Ascended Hosts hear your sincere call, a mechanism is activated which makes you return onto the Path. You forget in the hustle and bustle of your days that you took a responsibility upon yourself to follow the Path of Christ. However, all the conditions around you deepen and you enter a period of temptations and tests. And as you forget about your decision, every new test engenders discontent and fear within you. You start making appeals to God asking Him to lend you a helping hand in passing this dark period of your life.

And now imagine yourselves in the place of the Ascended Masters. How would you react if today you were asked for one thing, but tomorrow for something diametrically opposed?

Inconsistency and mood swings, and dependence on the surrounding environment are literally a scourge of your time.

You should develop in yourselves the basic qualities of a disciple: consistency, discipline, devotion, humility.

If you do not develop these qualities in yourselves, you will not be able to progress on the Path of discipleship and you will drop out of sight of the Ascended Teachers of humanity, as we will not be able to trace you amidst the chaotic flashes which we observe amid humans from our ascended state of consciousness.

Imagine a lighthouse which works today and does not work tomorrow. We orient by the burning fire of your hearts. When the fire on the altar of your heart keeps burning day and night without interruption and its brightness is smooth despite all the obstacles and ills of life, then angels can always trace you in the dusk of your world and give you help and support.

The main and basic obstacle which we meet amid the embodied humanity is inconstancy and the inability to be consistent in everything. For that reason, instead of feeling discontent and expressing displeasure to the Ascended Hosts, try to develop the basic qualities necessary for you on the Path.

At all times the qualities of constancy and persistence in achieving objectives have been highly recognised.

You need to sustain your aspiration, then the burning of the fire on the altar of your heart will be smooth and we will know that, right, this individual is ready to begin our work with him.

We consider not only the present moment, we are also perusing the Akashic records[5]. And we can judge how many times this individual decided to go on the Path of Initiations and how many times he took the wrong turnings from the Path. That is why each of you has your own waiting period for a Teacher who will come and get in touch with you. We see at a glance when you manifest the smooth burning of the fire of your hearts, but at times the Akashic records show that you started to follow the Path a few tens of times but

---

[5] **Akashic records** – the information field of the Universe in which all the events of the past, the present and the conceivable future are recorded. (Theosophical dictionary)

went off course. And then we are not allowed to work with you till the end of the current embodiment. However, this does not mean that you do not need to show readiness to follow the Path, because your aspiration and constancy will undoubtedly generate the momentum that will be needed in your next embodiment. This explains why some people can easily master our Teaching, being light on their feet and ready to gather and go where we point at our first call. Yet, other people read the Teaching, listen to the dictations, but at the next moment they are already fascinated by something else, and they thrust aside the books of our Teaching and run towards other nonsense or trinkets of your world.

Each of you is at your own level of consciousness. And as you live at the time of Kali Yuga[6], very few individuals are left in embodiment at your time that have certain spiritual achievements. Others are given a chance to go through re-education. And many of you go through this re-education for many embodiments. An opportunity is given to you again and again before the passage of the Divine opportunity closes. And when

---

[6] **Yuga** in Hindu philosophy is the name of a universal period or cycle. There exists Maha-Yuga (4 320 000 years) that consists of four shorter yugas or ages. These are the Satya yuga, the Dvapara yuga, the Treta yuga, and finally the Kali yuga. Their durations are at ratio of 4:3:2:1. The first of them is the Satya yuga, or the Golden Age, which is characterised by righteousness, wealth and universal thriving culture. The people of this age possess the most superior qualities, transcendent capacities, have huge height, strength and reason, they are very beautiful in appearance. During the second age – Dvapara yuga – the piety of the people decreases and the first signs of degradation of the society appear. During the Treta-yuga the piety decreases even more, though the people are still rather elevated and strong. The last age, Kali-yuga, is called the Iron Age or the Machine Age. It is the shortest (432 000 years), but the darkest of all the four yugas. This epoch is characterised by the universal moral decadency. There comes a time of the universal economical and spiritual degradation. Kali-yuga is the age which we live in. But in due time it will be changed by the Golden Age. (From the Encyclopaedia of esoterism)

you pass away and appear before the Karmic Board, you see your mistakes in horror and beg for one more opportunity and for one more embodiment. The mercy of Heaven is truly bottomless. And each of those who plead is given a new chance. But with every new embodiment the conditions become more involved. Your karma becomes densified and it is more and more difficult for you to get out of the viscous treacle of the imperfect thoughts and feelings in which the physical world lives for the most part.

Therefore, before repining at your unhappy lot and asking to be released from your karmic burden or to make it less burdensome, remember that you yourselves deserved in your previous lives everything around you and everything happening to you now. That is why sincere repentance and confession sometimes ease your karmic burden by half. God does not want you to suffer; it is you who devote yourselves to suffering. The understanding of your mistakes and the penitence give almost an immediate alleviation of your condition, and the burden lying on your shoulders lightens.

Today I have given you a Teaching on the Path and on why not everyone among you can follow this Path in this life.

I AM Jesus.

The Heavens give you one more chance

Beloved Quan Yin, June 27, 2009

I am Quan Yin, having come to you.

In the present context on the Earth there are very many moments which can play either a positive or a negative role in the course of the further process of evolution. I mean now that negative experience which many souls have accumulated in the course of the history of mankind.

Just look how the world has been balancing continuously on the verge of death during the last centuries. And the Ascended Hosts are staying in fighting trim all the time. Definitely, if you consider the history of humanity from the viewpoint of gaining spiritual experience, then, strange as it may appear to you, it is exactly this continuous balancing on the verge that has always given the souls an opportunity to get maximum growth and gives us, the Ascended Hosts, an opportunity to be co-participants in human history. Because whether human civilisation will continue to exist or not depends on to what extent we are able to act as a team at the critical moments of history.

Very many souls, when suffering and passing the hardest tests, were able to get free from the age-long karma which from the Divine point of view they deserved because of their incorrect behaviour in the past. And now, very many of those souls are helping humanity from the octaves of Light. That is why sometimes an absolutely damned soul, as it may seem by human standards, is able to transform and purify itself in a single moment. Yes, and exactly such is the opportunity available in the present situation on planet Earth. That is why I, as the Goddess of Mercy and

Compassion, come to every suffering individual at the first call and try to give the help that he/she needs. And sometimes one tender look of mine and a ray of Love emanating from my heart is enough for a soul, suffering in a terrible agony and dying, to resurrect for the new life. And very many people who are on their death bed and suffer from a serious illness, at the last moment with the last breath would be freed forever from the earthly suffering and revivified for the eternal life.

Everything depends on the state in which a person makes the transition, whether he feels anger towards the whole world or whether he is completely aware of the vainness of all his attempts to get satisfaction for himself and his soul from earthly pleasures and directs his eyes to Heaven and God.

At this moment of transition the soul transforms and ascends along the spiral of Life. That is why true believers have always helped incurables to make the transition and with this transition helped their souls to be granted the abolition of all the heaviness accumulated in their subtle bodies down the centuries. And this quality of your world - to regenerate the souls of people right from the ashes, dirt and rubbish - allows your planet to exist despite the monstrous distortions of the Divine energy across all the rays.

Today I have come to you in order to give your souls the knowledge about the path of transition. You can make the transition in your consciousness at any moment of your life on the Earth. That is the peculiarity of the current moment. You can get rid of the burden under the yoke of which humanity is moaning. The whole mechanism and the key to the alteration of your consciousness are hidden inside you. You only have to realise the new principles that are invariably to replace the old ones which the society currently lives up to.

You have to realise that such qualities as Love, Mercy and Compassion are not something abstract. These are the qualities that must become ingrained in the life of every person who wishes to continue the evolution on planet Earth. For you it is enough just to feel constant thirst and need for change. You must aspire with all your being to the future world, the world free of imperfections and vices inherent in mankind at this stage. And at that aspiration of yours the right patterns in music, architecture, new educational systems, health service and new economy systems will start to materialise in your world - the patterns which are already present and are constantly making their way into the consciousness of those individuals whose purpose of incarnation is to implant these models in the physical plane.

Humanity has got stuck in the old consciousness, the old life style. And when every person living on earth understands that it is impossible to live that way and that urgent changes and transformations are required, these changes and transformations, these right models in all the spheres of human life will start materialising here, there and everywhere on earth.

You just need to wish to give up that way of living that exists around you. Manifest your free will; verbalise your free will in your call to Heaven:

"Oh, Lord, I am tired of despair; I am tired of unfriendliness and gloomy faces of people. I want transformation! My soul is craving for renewal! My soul is tired and requires new energies to come, the energies of Love, Compassion and Mercy. Help, Lord, and accelerate the process of the transformation of planet Earth!"

As soon as sufficient numbers of individuals are ready in their consciousness, the changes will not keep the Earth waiting. The Ascended Hosts are ready for the transformation. All Heavens fasten their eyes on the Earth. Your turn is coming now. Can't you hear the call of time?

It is impossible not to notice the signs that are scattered about in the form of the weather conditions, in the form of cataclysms, in the form of the disorder in the economy and the financial sphere.

The time has come when the Heavens give you one more chance, and I announce this to you as a member of the Karmic Board.

I AM Quan Yin.

A Teaching on happiness and the Divine Path

Beloved Zarathustra, June 28, 2009

I AM Zarathustra!

I have come today to give a small Teaching. Our conversation will not tire you too much. I will be brief.

Today you will be given to understand to what extent everything that surrounds you can be changed and needs to be changed.

Imagine that you find yourself on a desert island. You have none of your habitual things; however, you remember, you bring to light from the bottom of your memory, the knowledge that you need in order to survive on this desert island.

Your civilisation has a great variety of things, and entertainment, and such toys for grown-ups, but in reality in order for you to exist you do not need so much. There is a basic minimum of things and it is enough. And if you think about it, after some brief contemplation you will understand that everything around you and everything you have does not make you happier.

So what is happiness?

For each of you the answer to this question will be different. And when you need to acquire something in order to be happy - a car, a flat, a country-house, an opportunity to travel or to get access to entertainment - then I have to tell you that you will never achieve happiness. This is because you will have to buy one thing after another, one toy after another, and you will strive to get more and more intricate pleasures of life. But every time you get the next thing or entertainment, you will immediately lose interest in it and will seek the next one to hunt for. And thus in this pursuit of the illusion many more than one or two incarnations pass away.

You are trying to find happiness outside of yourself. Yet happiness is the state of your consciousness. And when you are happy in truth, you need nothing, you are satisfied and ready to share your joy with the whole world.

How many of you have this state of inner happiness within your hearts? Doesn't it seem strange to you that the cheapest thing, even a free one is unavailable for the majority of the tellurians?

Why does it happen? It is because your civilisation sensitises people right from childhood to the acquisition and consumption of the blessings of civilisation. And there is no limit to more and more new things and pleasures your carnal mind wants to obtain.

Stop and think. Something is wrong in all this. There is a way out of this wheel in which you are running round from one embodiment to another like a hamster in an exercise wheel. And this way out is in your consciousness.

Stop and think. Your world obediently conforms to your consciousness. You get from the external world exactly that to which you aspire. Therefore, if you manage to change your consciousness, to alter the vector of your aspirations, then the matter, although slowly, will start changing and conforming the new level of your consciousness.

Start with the simplest thing, analyse: what is there from among your possessions that makes you happy? What can you toss away from everything you have?

Very many of you, after having thought, will say that you have nothing extra and that everything you have is necessary for your life. Remember the example of a desert island which I gave you at the beginning of our conversation.

You should aspire to a more simple way of living. And when your consciousness starts changing you will realise that you have a lot of free time which you did not have before. And you will develop a taste for healthier food, for more harmonious music. You will stop spurring yourselves with different stimulants in your rat race. You will understand that sexual activity is not love. You will make a lot of discoveries in your life. But first it is necessary to make a decision and to try to direct your consciousness towards the Divine Path.

You will say that you need to know the attributes of this Path and you need some signs of direction to where this Path is lying.

The sober fact is that all the direction signs are within you. And if you heed your inner voice carefully, you will soon know where the Divine Path lies.

Even those of you who do not have much faith in our messages and who are wary of various teachings and beliefs, even you have at least once in your life heard a hint from within yourself as to how you should act in a difficult situation that cropped up before you. You always know full well what to do and how to act. But then your carnal mind intervenes and whispers loudly: "Are you insane? It will be disadvantageous for you. What conscience? What dignity? You will lose your position (or something else from the mythical values of your world)".

And you keep listening to the human logic and miss a chance to act according to the Divine Law.

At fist sight, following the Divine Path does not provide any benefits in your world - neither money, nor fame. Quite the opposite, you forfeit much that is considered to be of high prestige in your world.

But you acquire other values. You acquire happiness, peace of mind and you become capable of experiencing the true feeling of Love.

You will not come across the direction signs of the Divine Path anywhere. But the compass and the map of the Divine Path are always present in your hearts from the very birth and until the transition. There is nobody outside of you who is to blame for your neglecting your inner knowledge and following the path that "everybody follows".

Do not strive to walk a broad road that leads nowhere. Walk along the narrow, hardly distinguishable path that leads you to the eternal life.[7]

I have said enough for those who are able to understand.

I wish you to jump out of your wheel and to find happiness!

I AM Zarathustra.

---

[7] Strive to enter in at the strait gate: for many, I say unto you, will seek to enter in, and shall not be able. (Luke 13:24)

A Teaching on Service

Beloved Djwal Kul, June 29, 2009

I AM Djwal Kul. I come extremely rarely through this messenger.

But today I have come as it is necessary to give you a certain Teaching. And I have volunteered to offer this Teaching for your attention. In reality there are very few people who have devoted their lives to the true Service. And I have come to give you the understanding of the true Service – not the service which you consider to be right, but the Service which is truly right.

Tell me, have you ever wondered about the notion of Service: what is it?

I think that you think more about the things of your world. Regretfully, Service is not a quality that is widespread in your world. And do you know why? It is because its very notion has been lost by your civilization.

I have come to rekindle Service. As soon as you ponder deeply over this subject, you will be able to get an idea about Service from the higher worlds. Your perception of the world continually makes you avoid thinking about more spiritual and eternal questions. However, the time has come when you should start thinking about the things that are not lying on the surface, but are necessary for you if you want to continue your progress on the path of evolution.

And so, Service. I know that very many people understand Service as the performance of some family duties which you discharge towards your relatives and those people who need your help. However, the concept of Service as it is meant by the Ascended Masters is much broader. In fact, the further evolutionary steps forward are impossible for humanity without Service. And next to the quality of Service there will also be a quality of unselfishness. It is because when you take upon yourself an obligation to perform some duties and wish to get something in return – any mortal thing of the physical world or a worthy place in the Divine world - this will not be a true Service.

In fact, Service is a state of your consciousness. It is following a certain order existing in this universe where every living creature serves other living creatures. And it is in this Concelebration that co-operation and development take place. Service is impossible without co-operation and true co-operation is impossible without Love. And now we have come to the alpha and omega of Service. True Service is possible only when it is based on the feeling of Love, but not Love in the same sense as you are used to thinking about it. You know about such forms of love as love towards a man or a woman, love towards children or parents. However, there exists greater Love as well - Love based neither on the attributes of kinship nor on gender. Love that is present within you as a state which no language is adequate to describe however much you try, but which saturates the entire creation. And when you in your consciousness reach the state of Love, Divine Love, you become capable of the true Service which you are told about by the Ascended Hosts.

Service to Life is like an indwelling being on the alert. You are constantly ready to fulfil your duty. Service also includes such qualities as responsibility and consistency. All the true Divine qualities have their concentrated expression in Service.

I must mention in particular the quality of humility that is indispensable in Service. At times you serve people who are in very heavy states of consciousness, and you need all your humility and patience in order to render such a person all the necessary help despite the manifestation of qualities of this person that are not the best. You should not be worried about the things you see in the physical plane. Caring for the soul, for the immortal part of an individual, should always be your primary concern.

At times you face a necessity to help a person, but unfortunately this person has been banging against a glass wall like a butterfly during his whole life and has lost his strength. Karma used to blur his eyes so greatly that he could not see the window of the Divine opportunity which was near and wide open for him.

The lives of the majority of the suffering human individuals resemble the picture of this butterfly which cannot find a way out. And if you approach an individual at the period of his great effort which he directs tirelessly but in the wrong direction, he will hardly hear you. But at the moment when his stamina is already leaving him there happens to be a moment of enlightenment at times and everything that you told him before can be heard even without words. It is because his soul has suffered enough and acquired special sensitivity during that suffering. At this moment you can render invaluable help to this afflicted soul, but unfortunately the result of this help will be seen only in the next embodiment. That is why true Service is sometimes manifested not in the daily sermons and admonitions, but in abiding the time when a soul opens like a rosebud and is ready to perceive the vivifying energy which you send from your heart into the heart of this individual.

These are very delicate points, beloved, and sometimes only a few seconds of a sincere prayer and support are enough when you send them from your heart to the heart of a person who needs help in order for his soul to be raised for the eternal life.

Do you feel the difference between the service when people pursue you with their preaching about the Word of God and the Service when you give a helping hand exactly at the moment when this help can be accepted and when it is more precious than millions of mistimed words?

One sometimes waits one's whole life for the moment when this kind of service can be administered to the soul of a person who needs help and is able to accept this help.

I have talked about the Divine Service with you today. And I will be glad if in the course of our talk you have received a piece of my Love that I have carefully delivered to you through the worlds.

I AM Djwal Kul.

The entire human community has entered the period of going through a collective initiation

Beloved Lanto, June 30, 2009

I AM Lanto, having come to you today. And the purpose of my coming today is to give you an instruction which, I hope, will be useful for you in your daily life.

Now when the cosmic cycles have changed, other qualities, other skills and abilities are required from you that are different from those that humanity had at its disposal in the past centuries. And the reasonable development of humanity in the future is not possible without mastering these new qualities and skills.

You may already feel it in yourselves now. We have warned you that the vibrations of planet Earth are rising onto a new level.[8] And in order for you to get used to these vibrations a rearrangement of the system of your world perception is required. This is a very complex and labour-intensive process. You should change your attitude to everything, and you should readjust the whole system of relationships that exists in your society.

This is not my initiative and it is still less an initiative of our messenger, it is what must happen inevitably because the survival of mankind is impossible without it.

Humanity as a whole must master new kinds of relationships. And these relationships must become of a character which is more close to the relationships which exist among us, the Ascended Masters. Why not follow our example and set aside your old poor-quality

---

[8] The dictation "**An important message**" by the Presence of the One, December 28, 2007 can be found in the appendix of this book.

relationships? To change your individualism to cooperation, your thinking only of yourselves to sharing your experience with the whole human family?

Do understand the time has come to move to relationships based on friendship, love, mutual help and mutual support. And no matter how you cling to the habitual stereotypes of behaviour, they will inevitably become things of the past, and dissolve together with those imperfections that are inherent in your society now: wars, acts of terror, epidemics and economic crises. Your society is sick and it is necessary to transit to the new level of consciousness and the new way of thinking in order to continue the evolution.

We are warning you for the reason that the general vibrational background on the planet is rising. And you have to follow this new level of vibrations. Everything that cannot adjust and change will be subject to a gradual purification. You should carefully observe yourself and the people around you. The same thing is happening now that used to happen when a person was going through initiations at secret schools of mysteries in the past.

To wit: this person was placed into conditions where the vibrations were of a higher level than that which was habitual for him. And all his bodies - the physical body and the more subtle bodies of the man - had to adjust to the new level of vibrations. The raising of vibrations pushes out of the person those negative energetic blocks that accreted with the individual and coexisted with him peacefully during many embodiments. That is why the person becomes predisposed to various negative states of consciousness, various pains in the physical body which cannot be qualified as usual diseases. His psyche goes through changes and he becomes nervous, unbalanced, gloomy and bad-tempered. Doesn't that look like a familiar picture to you?

But what happened in the schools of mysteries earlier referred only to one person or a group of individuals. Your planet and the entire human community have entered the period of going through a collective initiation.

Thus, you are given to understand that the passage of the cosmic opportunity is becoming narrower. It is high time for you to make the final choice: you either follow the Path of evolution or you become the tares, wastes.

You can tell me that the Cosmic Law is treating you inhumanely.

However, don't you act in the same way in your own kitchen-garden? You hoe up the weeds if they threaten your harvest. You cut the dead branches from the trees and burn them.

During the past millennia we have been continually coming to you through a great number of messengers and prophets. And we have been repeatedly warning you that it was necessary to align the course of development of your civilisation. It cannot be said that someone didn't hear about our warnings at least once in their life.

And the fact that we are implementing our changes in a smooth flowing manner gives you an opportunity to weigh everything one more time and to give the best part of you an opportunity to develop.

While there is yet time, think over my words. Weigh everything. Do not strive to solve everything at one stroke. Small yet continuous efforts that you apply in the right direction lead to the best results.

The karma you have created has interwoven the destinies of very many people with your own destiny.

That is why you cannot drop everything and rush to the forest or desert to save your soul. Every day you should apply efforts to transform your relationship with your relatives and workfellows. You should coordinate all the changes in your life with those people with whom you have the heaviest karma.

It is possible to turn the most difficult karmic situation into a favourable course, but for that you must devote all your life and, perhaps, not only one life, to untying your karmic knots.

Therefore, get ready for strenuous work upon yourself, upon your imperfections, and always remember that when you help someone to solve their problems, then, by doing so, you solve your own karmic problems. If you are sincerely glad about the achievements of somebody else, then, with this, you acquire the entire momentum of the merits of this person.

There are very many ways in which you can work off a very big karma in a matter of a few years, just by making correct choices and manifesting the right attitude to those situations which life provides you with.

I have given you an important Teaching which will be essential for you in these years and days.

I AM Lanto.

A Teaching on bridging conflicts

Gautama Buddha, July 1, 2009

I AM Gautama Buddha, having come through our messenger again.

It is a real gratification and joy for me to observe the faces of many of you at the moment when you are reading my dictations. A specific connection is being created during your attunement with me. When your vibrations rise at the time of reading our messages and harmony sets in, the higher world nears and literally enters your door.

Constantly keep this harmony, and many problems of your society will take care of themselves.

Trust me and my experience: the whole point is in the level of vibrations that humanity is able to keep up.

The topic of our conversation today is how to reach an understanding between people belonging to divergent movements. This concerns not only religious movements, but also movements in politics, in different social spheres of activity and in business.

It is seldom that peace and equilibrium hold sway over people. As a rule, the interests of people clash and this is a reason for conflicts and even wars. How to overcome the state of conflict and hostility which is inherent in your world and is one of its attributes at present?

It is not for nothing that I mentioned vibrations at the beginning of our conversation. Everything in your world is determined by the level of vibrations. And such a sphere as interrelation between people is also determined by the level of vibrations. What is this magic word that wars and conflicts and their happy resolution depend on?

It is very hard for me to explain this notion to you in those terms that you use and understand.

Picture a fish cast ashore. It is taken out of its usual environment and experiences the most difficult moments in its life. Each of you when finding yourself in a place, the vibrations of which do not match your vibrations, is like a fish washed ashore.

Every human represents a complex system. He consists not only of a physical body, but also of a less dense but still material substance. Everything is determined by the level of development of consciousness of a person. People differ from each other even at the level of DNA, at the level of their genes and chromosomes. Are you aware of these terms?

And so, every human bears in himself a certain energetic component. Every human has this or that inner potential enabling him to have this or that prevailing frequency which is natural for him.

For example, your body may determine the dominant frequency of vibrations. You prefer this or that food. And the food you like and eat determines your level of vibrations to a greater or lesser degree. For instance, if you eat meat or if you are omnivorous, it can be said with a high level of confidence that your vibrations are pretty low. The level of your vibrations is influenced not only by food, but also by your environment, clothes and the place you live in. In effect, you live in a particular place because your vibrations more or less correspond to this place.

However, your vibrations can change greatly in the course of your life. And when you decide to be a vegetarian, to give up smoking, drinking alcohol or listening to the wrong music, your vibrations start to alter, not overnight, but little by little. And you feel uncomfortable with your former relationships. It is as if you are expelled from the team you work in. The whole point is in the vibrations. You no longer match the average vibrations of all that surrounds you and this forces you to look for another job and other relationships.

Difference in vibrations lies at the heart of any conflict. You can say that karma lies at the heart of any conflict. But your karma is linked with your level of vibrations. And a human with a high enough level of vibrations has a considerable percentage of worked-off personal karma. But there are such notions as group karma, family karma, karma of a country and karma of a planet. And you cannot escape from working off these kinds of karma anyhow. And even if a person has reached certain results in working off his personal karma, he starts to "fall out" from the surrounding general vibrational background – and hence conflicts occur yet again.

And they are inevitable at a certain period of the development of mankind.

The vibrational difference at the subconscious level pushes you to make an unambiguous definition of who is close to you by vibrations and who differs from you. And if your vibrations are better-than-average, you are "pushed out" of the companionship like a ball pushed out to the surface by water.

So, conflicts are inevitable in society. Conflicts are inevitable as long as the society is at a very low vibrational level. But when the average vibrations of the human society rise, it leads to the accommodation of the conflict situations. First an opportunity opens up to avoid wars by means of negotiations and then the conflicts themselves stop having too negative a destructive character.

Human society has no other path except the path which you are taught by the Ascended Masters. You need not vindicate your convictions by force. The time is ripe for transition onto the next level of consciousness where any conflict can be resolved by every member of society through inner work upon himself.

If every member of society has no inner problems and no negative energy nestled in his aura, then no external stimuli and no external enemy can even approach you.

You are all pebbles lying on the shore of the ocean of the Divine Wisdom. And the incoming waves polish up your auras similarly to the newly arriving cosmic cycles. A certain number of cosmic cycles will pass and your auras will be of absolutely beautiful, gentle and clear colours.

All the shortcomings and all the imperfection can be surmounted. And there is a way to solve the problems of the human society. And that path is lying on the surface. And only laziness and disobedience inherent in people still make you suffer.

I have been happy to give this Teaching on bridging conflicts.

I AM Gautama Buddha.

A talk of vital importance

Beloved Kuthumi, July 2, 2009

I AM Kuthumi. I have come to hold discourse.

I would like to talk to you openly, earnestly and directly.

My heart wishes to talk to you about many things, but first of all, of course, about something that is of the most interest and the most value for you at this stage.

And the confusion that is present in your world is, of course, first of all caused by yourselves. First you perform irresponsible deeds, allow imperfect thoughts and feelings that seize hold of your being and then you are astonished at the effects your deeds, thoughts and feelings have.

The mental field of the planet is overloaded with your negative states of consciousness. The same takes place in the astral plane.

You hardly ever think about the impact that your thoughts and feelings have on everything that surrounds you. And in fact, all the negative effects that are present in nature, in the weather conditions, in the financial sphere and in any other spheres of life on planet Earth are generated by you yourselves. And some time later your own fruits materialise in the physical plane of planet Earth in the form of hurricanes, showers, drought or floods.

Many times we talked about the direct and immediate link that exists between your state of consciousness and everything that happens on planet Earth.

Your oblivion and constant hope that things will somehow come right by themselves make us, the Ascended Masters, doubt whether humanity is at all able to hear us and perceive the information which we give.

It seems that it has been said dozens of times that it is necessary to watch your thoughts and feelings, it is necessary to dedicate attention to the analysis of everything that happens to you during the day. It is just impossible to provide clearer signs in the physical plane. And the next step that is going to follow is a catastrophe of such a scale that you suspect but fear even to think about.

Why do you read our messages if you do not act according to our indications and requests in your life? It seems that humanity has come to the stage of its development when it is already unable to react to the information adequately.

In my dictations I have personally told you many times that you suffer from an excess of information. You overload your mind with different news and information that comes to you from different sources to such an extent that you not only become incapable of discerning the true information from the false, but now you do not react to any information. You just let it pass by, and everything that flows into your consciousness during the day cannot stay there a minute. The defence mechanism gets activated.

That is why I have come today to tell you one more time that you have to approach any information that you get very carefully. Even when it seems to you that the information passes by your consciousness it has an ability to settle in your subconscious mind. And you can never tell when and what kind of influence your subconscious mind will exert on you, your choices and your behaviour.

The genie of permissiveness and accessibility of any information has been let out from the bottle. And the only way out of this situation is to protect yourselves against everything that is unnecessary for your evolutionary development. And if you do not undertake steps in that direction, the next generation will not be able to react adequately to any information at all. Constant repetition influences your consciousness as coding. That is why you should expose yourselves to the influence of the modern mass media with great caution. The time has come when you have to separate the seeds from the tares in everything that surrounds you and reject everything that is not divine. I understand that when you are in the situation of constant pressure from the parts of all the modern advanced technologies which bombard your consciousness at full power via hundreds television and radio channels 24 hours a day, it is hard for you to find your bearings and understand how to act in this situation.

We teach you discernment and the right choices that you can make. And the first and most reasonable thing is to limit the influence of all the mass media on your consciousness and subconsciousness. When that pressure lessens, you will gain an ability to navigate and to distinguish. Your Higher Self, God inside you cannot talk to you; the Ascended Masters cannot talk to you while you are sealed off in the informational trash that is pouring out on you in tons from TV screens, radios, newspapers and the Internet during the day. You get a feeling that you are well-informed about all the latest events of the world, that you get information about all the innovations in all spheres. However, the main news that is not broadcast via any of your radio or TV channels is not available for most of the people of the Earth. And the main news is the SOS signal that your planet and everything that lives on it send.

You are like a mad captain that navigates a ship in a storm. The collective consciousness and the collective subconsciousness of humanity are like such a mad captain. And at any moment the ship, your planet, may strike sharp reefs and be shipwrecked.

You have tried, you have tasted all the fruits on planet Earth, and now the time has come when it is necessary to get back to the more subtle manifestations of existence. How can you hear the sounds of the music of my organ that I play every night in my retreat in the etheric octaves, if you are continuously deafening yourselves with all the background noise from your loud equipment?

To listen to silence, to the living voices of nature is tiresome and dull for you. You have created an artificial civilisation that has torn itself from everything that has been created by God on planet Earth.

I have come in order to try one more time to deliver the simple truths to your consciousness. And I become silent in the hope that, nevertheless, you have heard me.

I AM Kuthumi.

A Teaching on Maha Kranti

Beloved Babaji, July 3, 2009

I AM Babaji, having come to you today.

I have come today in order for you to get an insight into the stage at which humanity is now and into what is in store for you in the short run.

When I was incarnated[9] I was giving a Teaching on the great revolution - the great transformation in days to come – Maha Kranti.

Not all people who listened to that Teaching understood it. But everyone was afraid of the coming bloody events. I frightened them. However, the event that humanity is going to go through is not related to a revolution that could happen according to the will of people, a group of people, a political party or a country.

This revolution or transformation will happen by the will of the Higher forces. And its extent and the number of human losses that are inevitable in the coming change are determined by the level of consciousness that humanity is able to achieve now. Your level of consciousness is the only and crucial factor. You will either go through the coming changes or not. And those of you who are able to understand our Teaching and to follow it in your lives, you will be able to go through all the coming changes and nothing will impede you.

---

[9] **Shri Haidakhan Wale Baba (Babaji)** was a great spiritual teacher who lived from 1970 till 1984 in the Kumaon foothills of the Himalayas, the birthplace and home of many of India's great saints. He materialised in a cave near the village Haidakhan in the body of a young man. He devoted all fourteen years of his stay on earth to the service of the people in the ashram.

You should only understand the Teaching, pass it through yourselves, apply it in your lives, and your consciousness will change.

You cannot enter the future with the level of consciousness that most of humanity has now. And this is not just my whim; this is the law that exists.

When cosmic terms are nearing, the great transition, the great change inevitably happens. Humanity that is not ready for the transition in its mass will not be able to go through it. However, later conditions will be created on earth when new races of people will be able to inhabit the planet and continue the earthly evolution.

These changes always take place during the change of races. And these changes will unavoidably happen on the planet. However, you will not be told about the terms of these changes. The fixed dates are never given. The events that are inevitably coming are always spoken about. Each of you knows that the change is inevitable. And you all have a chance to change. You all have an opportunity to change your consciousness and follow the evolutionary path.

The previous great changes are described in the sacred books of the past. You have read about the Flood in the Bible, you have read about the great battle at Kurukshetra[10] in the Vedas.

Many historical documents of the past contain records of the changes that happened on planet Earth.

A very big number of souls are living on the planet now. And these souls, many of them, have the last chance to enter the evolutionary path of development.

---

[10] **Kurukshetra** is a place in India where the greatest war in the history of mankind took place. This war between Pandavas and Kauravas is described in the epic Mahabharata. Kurukshetra is a holy place of pilgrimage in Hindu, as it is thought that in this place Krishna gave the discourse of the "Bhagavat Gita" to prince Arjuna before the beginning of Kurukshetra battle.

The Teaching given by us will not be comprehensible for many of them. However, the question is not even in the understanding of the Divine Wisdom with the outer consciousness, the question is in following the inner law of purity and righteousness.

Your soul can be disgusting and from the outside you seem unusable for the evolution. However, the Karmic Board looks into the bottom of your soul and can discern under any layer of mud and many imperfections that golden glow which is impossible to hide from the experienced look of the wise men.

It seems to you that some man is unusable for further evolution because he is dirty, untidy and cannot settle in your life. But his soul is ready for further evolution. Another man has all the human dignity and honourable distinctions, he is surrounded by respect, glory, admirers, but he is not ready for further evolution - because his soul weltered in vice. The glorious of the world and the poor of the world. Among either of them there are those who will continue the evolution and those who will not.

There is no determinative feature that will tell the outer consciousness who is ready and who is not ready. Neither nationality, nor race, religious denomination, social status, age - nothing can be indicative of the ability to evolve or the inability to evolve.

There is no such criterion that would meet the human level of consciousness. However, for God the immortal spirit of some and the decay and stench of others is revealed under all human imperfections and faults.

That is why it is a very hard time in which you live. Everything is jumbled up and it is a hard job to discern and determine who is a valuable seed and who is a weed.

That is why there are so many temptations and so many things around at your time that do not conform to the Divine models.

If a soul is capable of the further evolution, no temptations of the outer world can lead that soul away from the Path. And those souls that are not ready, there is a chance for them to reject the surrounding temptations and follow the righteousness.

One cannot say that God is unjust. Everyone makes his choice on his own. And at the subconscious level everyone is aware of the choice he makes.

You yourself judge yourself and make a choice on your own. God does not impede you. And together with all the Ascended Masters I have an opportunity only to give these instructions, but these instructions are for those who are ready to hear them.

I AM Babaji. Om.

A Teaching on spiritual practices

The Great Divine Director, July 4, 2009

I AM the Great Divine Director.

One of the reasons for my coming to you today is to give you information concerning the work of the Karmic Board. We have completed our work. Both the result of our work and the decisions made by us cover the period until the next solstice - the winter solstice.

I will not keep it a secret that our work was not easy. And as always we were teetering on the brink. And our wish to give an opportunity to as many souls as possible to have one more chance and time for making a choice and a decision was taken into account by the Great Central Sun. That is why I am satisfied with the progress of work and with the decisions adopted.

With regards to your spiritual work and your directions of activity, I would advise you to think more over the fact that there is not so much time left. And the efforts of every human are needed now as never before, as sometimes the situation develops in such a way that the good teamwork of just a few lightbearers is enough for the preponderance of forces to be achieved on the side of prolongation of the evolutionary opportunity.

Many of you, very many of you think about what they could do in order to make themselves useful for the planet and for all the living creatures existing on it. Sometimes you take up meditative practices, at times prayer practices, and extremely rarely you try to do something in the physical plane. And I must tell you that any of your actions and any of your practices in the dual world can have a dual character. And two individuals doing exactly the same work and performing exactly the same actions may be working for different forces.

"How can it be possible?" you will ask me. And I will answer. The vector, the aspiration, the motive that lies at the beginning of your work or practice determines for the benefit of which forces all your actions and efforts will be directed.

I will give a concrete example from your life. You are trying to practise meditation. You know or you have read that it is very useful work. And you are trying to meditate. Meditations can be completely different. And some meditations touch only on the area of the mental plane. And this is the kind of meditation which should be taken up with extreme care, because the mental plane is close to the earthly plane. And any deviation of your thoughts in the negative direction during the meditation or before the beginning of the meditation leads to a directly opposite effect.

For example, you wish to work with your thought for the benefit of all the living creatures, and you strive to elevate your thought and to direct it for the good. But at that moment some problem that exists in your family or at work comes to your mind. Your thought strays from the predetermined theme of the meditation by a hair's breadth. You do not even notice this. However, you alloy your negative state into the course of the meditation. And if many people take part in this meditation - tens, hundreds or maybe thousands of people - and each of them introduces his negative moment into the common course of the meditation, it can happen that the whole course of the meditation will take a directly opposite direction and the result of it will be directly opposite to the result you expect.

We know that such a thing is possible and takes place frequently. That is why we come up to collective meditations with extreme care and extremely rarely ask you to take them up. The force of thought and the aspiration of thought for the majority of people are not their strong suits. That is why meditations, even if they are not held in the required state of consciousness, cannot exert a big negative influence, but you should learn to approach everything very consciously - and especially now when the worlds are nearing each other.

Your spiritual practices can do both harm and good. Everything depends on the state in which you start your spiritual practices.

And I must mention also that by misdirecting your energy during the spiritual practice you create the same kind of karma as by performing any wrong action in the physical plane.

Yes, beloved, the time has come for you to think before sending up a prayer: are you not creating karma with this prayer?

The right state of consciousness during the prayer and the right attunement during the prayer are essential elements[11]. The words of the prayer which you use are also very important. Be mindful of the words of the prayer. And if you do not understand what this prayer is about, you cannot forward the energy of prayer accurately.

There is a practice of reading mantras. It is a special practice. And, as a rule, you do not understand the sense and the meaning of mantras. It is the very vocal sounds of mantra that have an impact. However, here

---

[11] You can also read more about the importance of achieving the right state of consciousness during the prayer practice in the dictation "**All the sense of the prayer-practice is in the raising of your consciousness**" by Padma Sambhava, April 23, 2005, which can be found in the appendix of this book.

you are also encompassed with perils, because if you pronounce mantras incorrectly, the effect from your practice of reading mantras can be negative too.

This Teaching is being given to you now with a hope that you will use spiritual practices and spiritual techniques more cautiously. And if even the verified spiritual practices can have a negative impact, then what kind of impact can those practices that you yourselves invent and disseminate have? If a spiritual practice offered by you is incorrect from the Divine viewpoint and you have disseminated this practice among a fairly large number of people, the karma created by these people as a result of using your practice will fall fully on your shoulders.

That is why I would caution you against showing broad initiative, especially in mass media, regarding the introduction of new practices and techniques. It is not by accident that in ancient times all the spiritual practices and techniques were disseminated by way of disciplic succession and the Teacher kept strict watch on how a spiritual practice was followed by his disciples.

You think that you have achieved considerable heights in spiritual development and you yourselves can teach and preach. Well, nobody including myself can forbid you to do so. But we are obliged to give the Teaching on spiritual practices. You can either use this Teaching in your lives or not. However, I hope very much that many of you will be very careful when taking up spiritual practices, especially those from among the newfangled ones.

I have warned you and shown you the right direction on your Path.

I AM the Great Divine Director.

There is a likelihood that the Golden Age will come to the Earth

Master Hilarion, July 5, 2009

I AM Hilarion.

The subject of our talk today is such notion as making a Divine decision in your lives. In our messages you probably could have read that all your actions and thoughts should correspond to the Will of God. However, many of you wonder how to puzzle out what exactly amidst all the chaos around you does correspond to the Will of God and what does not, which decision is a Divine one and which is not.

As always, the basic and the main recommendation will be to heed the voice of your heart, as it is exactly there where the answer to all your questions is located.

But what can those who do not hear the answers do?

Regretfully, in the course of many embodiments on the Earth the hearts of very many people have been cased in impenetrable armour and it is very difficult to hear the answer of God through this armour.

You have faced very many tragic situations in your lives. These tragic situations have lacerated your hearts and the wounds are now sore and aching even under that layer of armour in which you have clothed your hearts just not to feel this pain.

What can be done? Your hearts need to be restored to a serviceable condition. You should layer-by-layer peel off your hearts all those adverse influences which took place in the past and also exist in the present. Your heart is very sensitive, and so before learning to open your hearts it is necessary to take care to make sure that the external conditions of your life would not inflict new wounds to your hearts.

Regrettably, there are many things in your world that make your hearts shrink from intolerable pain. It was not always like that.

There were happy ages in the history of mankind when people were happy for each other, enjoyed the sun, were jubilant over all the living creation. Joy was the fundamental quality. This was long ago. This was in ancient times when civilizations of the Golden Age existed on the Earth.

The best representatives of mankind and their Teachers were incarnated at that time. The nature and everything around represented a harmonious manifestation of divinity. Everything existing at that wondrous time was happy. The states of happiness and joy were the dominant states of everything alive. The relationships between people were equally perfect and filled with Love. Everything was organised reasonably.

And in those centuries the hearts of people did not need to be covered with impenetrable armour. The hearts of people were open to everyone because there were no negative manifestations. And the hearts of people always knew how to act in harmony with the Divine law.

This was a very long time ago.

Humanity has gradually slid into the state in which it is now. Everything that surrounds you in your life corresponds to the state of your hearts. And the armour of misunderstanding, hatred and dislike is enwrapping mankind.

You have tasted the fruit of disobedience to the full. After all, it is exactly your self-will and the wishes to obtain something for yourself that have led mankind to this state of consciousness in which it is now.

So, the return journey from this state will be the demonstration of precisely the opposite patterns in all the spheres of life.

Hatred must be superseded by Love.

Fear must be ousted by Love.

Indifference, spite and enmity should be substituted by friendliness.

Joy must replace sullenness.

All the non-divine qualities are superseded by the Divine ones as if touched with a magic wand, but only if the majority of mankind replaces its way of behaviour posited on egoism, vanity and the wish to continually receive the pleasures of life, with the way of behaviour posited on mutual help, co-operation and a wish to give everything to life.

You will be right if you say that I am speaking about the standpoints based on egoism and altruism.

At the time when human consciousness slides away from Divine vibrations, in this case a human separates himself from God, he no longer feels secure, he stops experiencing Love. When a person returns to Divine vibrations a directly opposite process takes place. This person experiences his unity with the entire Creation, feels Love and joy. He is satisfied, quiet and good-tempered.

The boarder of the Divine world is in your hearts. It is there where, under the layer of armour, God resides. And when every human becomes able to open his heart, the entire humanity will return to the times when people on earth were constantly experiencing a state of happiness and Love.

There is a likelihood that these times of the Golden Age will come back. There a likelihood that the Golden Age will come to the Earth. And we are waiting and wondering where the conditions necessary for the advent of the Golden Age will be created on the Earth.

I will not be telling you about our plans. But you should know that it is not always that the sky is dull and it is raining. The time will come when the sun of the Divine consciousness will lighten the Earth. I can only say that the conditions needed for the advent of the Golden Age are already being created now, and those souls who bear in themselves the consciousness of the Golden Age are preparing for embodiment and are already coming into embodiment. And it would be good if you could create for these souls such conditions on the Earth in which they would be able to manifest their talents and abilities in full.

I am finishing today's message hoping that you will be able to find strength in yourselves and to overcome your negative states for the sake of the future of planet Earth.

I AM Hilarion.

A Teaching on the right use of the Divine energy

Master Godfre[12], July 6, 2009

I AM Godfre.

I come extremely rarely through this messenger. And taking the opportunity of today I would like to address the wide audience of lightbearers of the whole world.

I incarnated in America, and today I come through a Russian messenger. The very fact of my message today speaks for itself. There are no contradictions between individuals when they reach a certain spiritual level of their development.

When you are in lowland you can see mountains in the distance, but you do not have a wide view. When you climb to the top of a mountain a landscape opens before you that you could not see while you were in the lowland. So your task is not to twiddle-twaddle and not to get stuck in the swamp of everyday vanity. Your task is to raise yourself in your consciousness as high as possible to the sphere where there are no contradictions between people.

Differentiation in your world exists only because you have not reached that level of consciousness from where the wide horizon of the Divine Freedom is opened.

I spent my last incarnation in America. And I love that country very much. And I am also glad that I can

---

[12] Ascended Master **Godfre** incarnated as Guy W. Ballard, the messenger of Saint Germain. The teachings of the Great White Brotherhood and the Law of the I AM Presence came to earth through him. He was keeping the focus of Christ consciousness for the planet till his ascension in the year 1939. His wife Edna Ballard is now Ascended Lady Master Lotus. Guy Ballard wrote under the pseudonym Godfre Ray King.

come through the Russian messenger because the relations between these two countries should be maintained.

The spiritual development of Russia can give much to America. And the experience of America can be adopted by Russia as well.

There is a Divine solution to any problem and contradiction in the physical plane. And when there is a sufficient number of ardent hearts ready to kindle thousands of lightbearers with their own example, then any ice, any coldness of relations between any countries of the world will melt.

It is necessary to rise above politics, above economics, above any human spheres of relations.

I will reveal a very big secret to you. And this secret should be told to as many people as possible. Immediately! This secret is that as soon as you let God be present in yourself, you change everything around you.

You, each of you, let God be present within you! Invite your I AM Presence to enter your temples and to stay in them constantly.

There is a divine spark within each of you. That is why each of you can make your physical temple a place of the constant presence of God. You can expand the presence of God in you only as much as your physical and more subtle conductors can bear.

All the spheres of human life are determined only by the extent to which people let God be present within them.

This is a very simple truth. And this is just what you need to do every day - to invite your I AM Presence to your temple.

This is the simplest practice and the simplest spiritual technique that may ever be.

You say:

"In the name of I AM THAT I AM, I invite my I AM Presence, a divine spark within me, to be with me throughout this day. I ask you, my I AM Presence, to take under your immediate control all my actions, deeds, words, feelings and thoughts. I ask you, my mighty I AM Presence, to act through me throughout this day, to guide my life. Amen."

And after your call the presence of God in you will be reinforced as much as your four lower bodies may allow. You will become a conductor of Light for your world.

Your world needs Light. Your world experiences a lack of energy. You should use your Light with great care. You are responsible for the Light that you give to the people around you.

There are people who need your Light, your energy, as a drink of water in a hot desert. And your energy will give them an opportunity to have a rest and wend their way through life again. But other people want only to take and get your Light, they do not want to do anything themselves and, moreover, they use the received energy not for Divine purposes but for the purposes opposite to the Divine. In such a case the karma of their misuse of the energy falls upon you. You are responsible for the Light that you give. And you should use it correctly in your lives.

One does not water a dry tree. And one does not water weeds. But something that is alive that yields well should get its portion of reviving water.

I have given you a Teaching on the right use of the Divine energy in your lives.

Idle talk, endless bickering - all this makes you use the Divine energy incorrectly.

God gives you energy so that you could energise those who are in need, who need your help and support for further wending through life.

I have given you a Teaching on the careful use of the Divine energy. But only you yourselves can and must put this Teaching into practice in your lives.

I AM Godfre.

A serious talk with the people of Russia

Master Nicholas Roerich, July 7, 2009

I AM Nicholas Roerich.

I have come through this messenger for a serious talk which we will have today.

There is not so much time left - the time of the Divine opportunity that is open before the world.

And Russia is to be the key player in this opportunity.

You know how my heart always ached for Russia when I was in incarnation. And now my heart is constantly concerned about Russia. I am still deeply attached to Russia with all my thoughts. And I feel the load of responsibility lying on me.

If I were in incarnation now, I could do so much living in Russia. So many opportunities have opened up before you. There were no such opportunities in the time of my embodiment. I was not even able to be present in the territory of Russia and had to live most of my life outside of it.

You live in Russia now. You have colossal opportunities at your disposal. I wonder - why do you do nothing? Where are those men who saved Russia in the terrible times of invasion of foreign hordes in ages past?

Can it be true that the Russian land has been impoverished to such an extent that there is no chance to unite under a great idea of unification of all the forces of Light and all the lightbearers of Russia in order to contradistinguish Russian values and Russian culture from the foreign culture and values? Russian culture has always been one of the most human and humane in the world. Russian composers and artists have reflected glory upon this great country in not-so-old times. Why has the Russian land been depleted?

Why are money and material values running the show? How long will you be enjoying this strange way of life? Isn't it time to return to the true values?

Hasn't the time come to bring to mind dignity and honour?

Hasn't the time come to bring up children in the devotion to the common timeless values of mankind? Look at what your youth is doing. Should it be like this?

I am sad to watch this picture of the general decay and corruptibility.

I am trying to work with the other Ascended Masters on awakening the souls of the Russian lightbearers from their lethargy. I am trying to find those representatives of the intelligentsia for whom the very notions of honour, dignity and motherland have not yet become devalued. I am trying to find those souls.

Yet more and more I surrender to despair. Even when I manage to find a soul who is awakening to the Truth and for which everything becomes subordinate to Faith and God, some time passes and this soul gradually leaves the Divine path and starts seeking some mythical values and some surrogates of culture.

There are so few souls left that are really devoted to the highest ideals of spirituality. There are so few of those among them who have not burdened themselves with karma and are able to perform the deeds of the Masters in the physical plane.

I think with horror about the fact that there are so few devoted fellowmen in embodiment now who have not lost their bearings and have not lost direction.

You are the ones I am mostly appealing to today. The victory was always gained not with numbers, but with talents.

That is why it is necessary to create a united front against that platitude that has flooded the life in Russia today.

So many beautiful souls who have come into embodiment to fulfil a mission of Light are now netted into the web of this platitude and permissiveness.

It is time to summon all citizens to arms as it was in the time of Minin and Pozharsky[13] for the confrontation with the enemy that has taken over Russia from the part of the subtle plane of thoughts and feelings. It is time to set the Divine patterns in everything against everything non-divine which is running the show at present.

Today's rouble, if invested into the right upbringing of the growing generation, will be repaid a thousandfold and the spiritual riches of Russia will increase in the future.

And the point is not even in material inputs, but at times a simple manifestation of the best qualities of the soul is enough to sow good seeds in the souls of children.

Your smile doesn't cost anything, your love doesn't cost anything, your friendliness doesn't cost anything. God gives you all that. And you must bring all this to the world.

The whole problem is in the fact that you have forgotten about God, about the fact that you have come to this world to carry on the deeds of God, but not to indulge the fancy of your ego, your carnal mind.

---

[13] Prince **Dmitry Pozharsky** and merchant **Kuzma Minin** became national heroes for their role in defending the country against the Polish invasion in the 17th century. They gathered the all-Russian volunteer army and expelled the Poles from the Moscow Kremlin, thus putting an end to the Time of Troubles in 1612. (translator's footnote)

I have not come to give you a message for a long time because I was managing to contain my indignation. It is improper for me to worry so much. I'm sad for the country, I'm sad for the nation, I'm sad for the people who lead an aimless life sitting in front of their TVs or with a glass of vodka.

Shame on you, men!

Every day in my prayers I am asking for the Divine opportunity to be prolonged for Russia for some more time to allow the country to finally shake off its aimless life and fondness for the pursuit of money and gain. True values exist! There exists something for the sake of which you have come into embodiment and to which your everyday efforts must be directed.

I have come for a serious talk with the residents of Russia and with those its citizens who have left for other countries in search of a good and easy life.

Believe me, when you pass away, you will be surprised to remember the days of your embodiment spent senselessly and you will be ashamed of the decisions you made that give you goods of the physical world but at times close the Kingdom of Heaven for you forever.

I AM Nicholas Roerich.

A talk about the qualities necessary for the further evolution

Padma Sambhava, July 8, 2009

I AM Padma Sambhava, having come to you through the worlds.

The topic of our talk today will be an eternal theme that will stay relevant as long as the manifested worlds exist. This is a topic of a Teacher and a disciple, a Guru and a chela.

You have access to the most modern means of mass media; you have at your disposal such means as the Internet; you have mastered the computer. But I have to tell you that your civilization has not advanced an inch in the relationships that are in place for as long as the manifested worlds exist.

On the contrary, you think that you know everything and that you can get access to any information that exists in your world in abundance.

You are assured that all the information can be bought for money and is either lying on the shelves of shops or can be received by attending a workshop.

You are led into a delusion and you are mistaken as the information that is really valuable will not lie on the shelves of shops.

No matter how your civilization wants to get access to this information, it cannot get it, because in reality all the keys to any information are hidden inside you. And in order for you to obtain these keys you should raise your consciousness up to the level at which you are allowed to get these keys. The mechanism for teaching the Divine wisdom has been elaborated during centuries. And it is in the way that a disciple is waiting humbly for the moment to come when the door behind which the Truth is hidden will be opened slightly.

Time has changed. But it has changed only in the sense that less and less people are able to obtain the qualities which lead to the door behind which the Truth is hidden. The rest search for the Truth not in the place where it lies, but in the places where mass media spotlight it and where the trumpets blare that – here it is – the Truth.

Quietly, very quietly the realisation of the Truth comes. Between two breaths and between two beats of the heart.

No, the noise of the street and the noise of mass media are not suitable for the beginning of the search for the Truth.

There is too much hustle and bustle in your civilization. And when someone proclaims the next nonsense presenting it as new information that has just arrived from the higher spheres, one may smile, but one also may be saddened. Because there is much hustle and very much of everything but there is no Truth.

The heaven-sent threads like spidery lace are scattered in your world as signs leading to the retreats of the Truth. But you do not notice the signs and do not pay attention to them.

You should start doing very simple things in order for your civilization to gain at least a rough idea of those subjects that are related to the secret knowledge that is still being disseminated on earth by way of disciplic succession.

Never, not even in the toughest times has the link between the worlds been torn. Even in the most terrible times there were always people in embodiment who were bearing the vibrations of the Truth to the world.

There are special places on earth where the bearers of this Knowledge, this Truth are present.

I know, I am sure that the time will come when people will become tired of the hustle, when people will start returning to that narrow path that leads to the Truth.

When I was in embodiment I did not start a conversation with someone who was striving for knowledge until he demonstrated his aspiration and humbleness.

At times I was waiting and watching for ten years before starting the simplest talk with these individuals who strived to become my disciples in order to gain a piece of the Truth.

Who of you can sit in the pose of meditation and wait humbly for the moment when your vibrations will allow the Teacher to talk to you?

No, you want to pay money and to get all the knowledge for your money.

Calm down. Truth and knowledge are not bought for money. They enter your being when your consciousness is ready to perceive them.

This happens inevitably. Once the cup is ready – the Teacher comes. This is the law that is in place in your physical world.

And if you approach the Teacher before you are really ready, you will feel nothing but disappointment. And what is more, you will accuse the Teacher of all those imperfections that are inherent in you. It is because a genuine Teacher is a mirror in which you see yourself.

It often happens that people consider the time and the circumstances of the physical world to have changed so much that new approaches and new teachings are necessary and that the old approaches have become obsolete and are not relevant any longer.

Well... Probably it is so for you. However, the laws that have been operating in the universe for billions of years have not changed yet.

One day your scientists will find the confirmation of the cosmic laws in their labs. But this will not happen before the consciousness of mankind is ready to accept these discoveries. But until that time comes science will remain separated from the Truth, just as your civilization as a whole is separated from it.

I have come to you today so that you can make it clear in your consciousness that until you work out in yourselves the qualities necessary for the further evolution you will not advance an inch from the still point where mankind has been milling about for a few millennia already.

I will repeat these qualities for a better understanding.

You need humility before the Higher Law, you need aspiration, obedience, patience and tolerance.

These are the main qualities.

You also need the right vector which will give the right direction to your progress on the Path. But the right vector is considered to be a wish to help all the living creatures existing in this universe.

I have given you an instruction. And you need time for pondering now.

I AM Padma Sambhava. Om.

I invoke your consciousness heavenward

Beloved Mother Mary, July 9, 2009

I AM Mother Mary having come to you.

Since the time of our last meeting such events have happened that have caused the postponement of the advent of the New Age which is still expected to come to Russia.

We have encountered resistance on the part of the opposing forces that craftily manipulate some individuals and act through them.

I have been always aspiring to strengthen my presence in Russia. And I am vexed by everything that is taking place.

I am not saying that everything is bad. I do hope that everything will go well. But you need to channel your energies. You need to maintain a certain level of effort every day to reach those blessed times that are to come to Russia.

I have begun my message on a sad note. But you yourselves feel that not all is as we would like it to be, and I will add: "Not the way it was conceived".

However, we will not wait and let the grass grow under our feet.

Isn't it right that if I ask you to double and triple your efforts you will respond to my call?

And for some people this will mean an intensification of their prayer effort, others will get down to the performance of concrete actions in the physical plane.

You can do a lot. And if you regularly heed the pieces of advice we give you and also that soft voice which is cutting its way from your heart through the hustle of your day, we will be able to do very much and in the shortest possible term.

Now it is necessary to gather all forces for the decisive dash. Right now it is being decided whether the expected changes will come and how fast they can come first to Russia and then to the whole world. I will not let you in on the details and this is not my place to show someone which steps he/she should take. Everyone should do his own job. And I am running my ministry day and night continually in the higher plane.

I am as close to the earthly plane as it is possible to be. And every day I listen to all your requests and even reproaches which you send to me.

I am ready to hear from you even some not very pleasant things that you sometimes tell me. At times in order for you to realise something you must hear it yourselves. And when you are saying it to me, you hear it yourselves. The problems of many of your embodiments have stuck deep inside you.

You come up to my image and start your inner monologue. It never occurs to you that I hear every single word you are saying. And when the Divine opportunity permits I immediately send angels to help you. The help comes immediately in the higher plane. And a certain time is necessary for this help to be materialised in your physical plane. But sometimes you do not wait long enough for this help to come and send me your reproaches and express your dissatisfaction. And immediately the flow of the Divine opportunity stops. And next time when you come up to my image repenting and weeping, I render my help to you again. But then everything recurs. And when you ask about one and the same thing for the fifth or seventh time, then I do not hurry to help you, because you have not realised the whole responsibility with which you burden the angelic hosts by each of your requests.

Be consistent in your requests and actions.

Sometimes your karma does not let me intervene into your destiny, but you ask me for help every day, many times a day, for a year or even longer. And then your effort and aspiration break the invisible barrier and help flows into your being and into your life as an extensive stream.

The Divine mercy does not know limits. And the help will come from the higher plane. Learn to use this help. Don't cut the Divine opportunity with your negative rushes. If you could keep attunement with the Divine world most of the time, how much easier it would be for us to render help to you and how much more successfully we could progress in the transformation of the physical plane of planet Earth. Every time you lose equilibrium you are like a small volcano. And everything thrills around you, and the elemental life longs to go away from you because your vibrations do not let elemental beings come near you.

And when you turn on loud music with broken rhythms, elementals and angelic beings flee headlong from the zone where this terrible music can be heard. The equilibrium is shattered to such an extent that during several days after such music sounded in some zone none of the beings whose responsibility is to put things right in the higher plane can enter that zone. And since you turn on music every day, your towns and settlements are like deserts now: all the inhabitants of the higher plane have left these deserts and cannot help you.

We help you mostly through the elemental kingdom, through the elements of air, fire, water and earth. With your behaviour you deprive us of an opportunity to give you a helping hand.

We need to have a harmonious atmosphere in the physical plane. And in those places on earth where an atmosphere of peace and balance still reigns you are healed even when you simply get into such places. Thousands of beings of elemental life are ready to render healing and help to you.

So think – hasn't the time come already to return to the harmony between all the kingdoms of nature that reigned in days gone by when people were happy and felt the joy simply of being? At that time they saw elemental life, saw angels, and this was as natural as it is now for you to see dogs, cats and birds.

I invoke your consciousness heavenward. I am trying to bring home to you the fact that you live in a cage and that you have encaged yourselves with your own hands and have put this cage in the desert of your cities.

The time is ripe to reconsider the whole system of values and all the relationships in all the spheres of life. How is it possible to bring home to you that you live in inhuman conditions?

Be brave to give up your affection to the "blessings" of your civilisation, and you will gain genuine blessings and lasting values.

Nature abhors a vacuum, and each of your negative qualities will be replaced by a Divine one and your human affections will be replaced by a state of Divine peace, harmony, tranquillity, happiness and joy. And this is exactly what you lack in your lives.

Today I have tried to direct your eyes higher than your habitual horizon to enable you to see the heights you should be aiming for now.

I AM Mother Mary.

We continue the mission that we have started in Russia

Master Morya, July 10, 2009

I AM El Morya.

Have you been waiting for me? I know that very many of you have been anxiously waiting for my coming since none of the Masters speaks so decidedly and concretely as I do.

And the responsibility for the whole mission that we are starting in Russia rests on me. And my responsibility makes me speak succinctly, concretely and to the point. It is necessary to discuss a lot within the limits of one message.

So, I will start then. You might know that our mission in Russia is stuck. And you may know that the reason for that is the sluggishness of those lightbearers who were to be involved in our mission but instead found other activities for themselves and started doing something that is far from our interests.

For what a long time and how thoroughly our missions of Light are prepared! How many discussions are held in the higher plane with the souls preparing for those missions.

And once you approach the time when actions are needed something that is impossible to programme beforehand happens: you are carried away by something that you were never interested in before and believe that you have incarnated precisely for that. You do not hear and do not want to hear any of our words that you read in the messages or hear in the retreats during your nightly dreams; you do not see any signs in the physical plane, you are just caught up in the illusion.

So what is left? I applaud the heroic efforts of our messenger. It will not be a secret to you if I say that it was not in the least planned that this woman would be involved in the construction and would dedicate the invaluable days of her incarnation to the things that were to be done by other people.

I applaud, but at the same time I have to say all fine and dandy, but instead of advancing forward during those two years while the construction was in progress we have stepped several years back.

Yes, we are forced to put you at a desk of the first class and start our training again instead of doing those things that have been planned.

We expected to make greater progress, but we will not put the cart before the horse. We will be waiting until the Russian man has got enough sleep and half-rises from his stove-bench.

There is a proverb: "The Russians harness slowly but drive fast". I have to say that you have not even started to harness yet.

We are right at the beginning of the path and are urgently seeking replacement for those individuals who volunteered to take part in this mission of Light but did not stay the distance. Each person has his own reason, but the overall result is deplorable. Isolated lights, flashing here and there, cannot serve as an indicator of success. And instead of rallying under the banner of our messenger you have found a pretext for yourselves in the form of different assignments that you try to undertake in the physical plane here and there.

There cannot be any other assignments for you than those of the Brotherhood.

And when we sound full-blast the full-scale attack, you cannot be playing the harmonica. But that is exactly what many things you do look like.

Instead of taking part in our mission and helping us, you have found many activities that are perhaps good at a certain stage of evolutionary development but in no way suitable for your souls.

It is the same as if an alpinist who has conquered many of the highest peaks of the world will be climbing an ice-hill down which five-year-old children slide in winter. I do not know what other words I can find to reason with you.

But nevertheless we continue the mission that we have started in Russia. We will be moving just as much as will be possible. I am sad. We could have achieved much more.

However, it is early to strike the balance; the work is quite far along. And when we are able to unfurl our banners and deploy our troops, we will see who will dare to set off their ingenious ploys and mercantile interests against us.

The time has come to build up our power in the physical plane.

We say time and again that it is necessary for you to perform concrete actions, and to perform them not chaotically but in an organised way. Becoming a union is necessary for you. As soon as we can implement what we planned in one place of the globe we will be able to easily repeat that experience in many places.

I expected more promptness and vim of you. Well, we will try to restructure our battle lines and continue augmenting the potential of Light. You have been waiting a long time for my coming. However, I cannot afford the time to talk to you for long.

Do work better, and I will devote more time to you!

I AM El Morya.

The statement of Lord Shiva

Lord Shiva, May 24, 2009

I AM Shiva!

I have come! I have to make a statement, and I would like you to hear with great attention and respect everything I want to bring home to you.

First of all you should make a certain effort to free yourselves from the influence of the illusion surrounding you. You speak with God, so in your minds and hearts only Love and Gratitude to God and the Supreme Law should be present.

You and God. How often can you be face to face with God and speak with Him?

I think the experience of our communication today will compel you to take your mind off your illusion and speak with God more often.

Don't think that God would come up to you when you are sunk in hustle and bustle. Don't think that you will manage to hear the voice of God when you are plunged in your human activities.

There is a considerable difference between the plane in which you reside and the plane in which I reside. And in order for you to approach me you should steep yourselves into my world. You will be able to understand me only when you manage to raise your vibrations up to the level where I can reside. Therefore, I have come to you now in order to remind that there is not much time left at your disposal. You must approach with all responsibility the fact that considerable changes are taking place on the planet. And these changes will no longer allow you to live the same way as mankind has been living up to date.

Nothing that surrounds you in the physical world matters a bit in the spiritual world. And I have come to call you to the spiritual world in which absolutely different values exist. Do understand that as long as you are attached to the illusory world you are not able to progress higher. And those of you who are ready in their consciousness for the contact with the Higher worlds – you have nothing to be sorry about and nothing to fear, because your souls are ready for the transformation and will enthusiastically acclaim the changes which are to come. I have no worry about you. But there are souls who are not ready for the transition, who are lazy about changing their consciousness and hesitate to change themselves. They do not even hurry to get rid of such habits as smoking, eating meat and drinking alcohol. How many of you are dependent on such things...

You will not be able to transit to the New world and to keep your attachments. It is exactly you to whom I have come to appeal this day. You have to understand that there is no time left. The leap into the new world can arise at any moment. Do not throw into the scale God and Mammon and do not try to figure out in advance how the things will go and how everything will take place. It is not given to you to understand the plan of God with your human consciousness. You must only obey God's Law and follow Him dauntlessly.

Because for you it is the only way out of the corner into which you have painted yourselves. It is to you that I am appealing and it is you whom I am giving one more chance.

Stop fussing about, stop running and rushing about. Your state of consciousness will determine your future -

your state of consciousness which you will manage to keep in peace, notwithstanding what is happening now and what will be happening around you.

As to my devotees, I would like to ask them to read the mantra "**OM NAMAH SHIVAYA**". But since there are few true devotees of mine left in the world, the best way out for you is to keep the highest state of consciousness accessible for you. You can find your immortality and the transition to the New world only when keeping the inner devotion to God and the Supreme Law.

Those of you who are grinning while reading my message and feel doubt and criticism inherent in your carnal mind, I will not be bail you out. And your salvation I leave to your own hands. There are not many people left in the world who must and can be saved. The rest are making their choice themselves or have made it already.

The cosmic terms, no matter how long they can seem to be from the human level, still have their beginning and their completion.

Therefore, today, the same as a month ago[14], I have come with the only goal – to give you an opportunity to get out of the web of the illusory world and to open the door to the Divine world.

The time has come now. Tomorrow it may be too late.

I AM Shiva, I have said everything!

---

[14] The speech is about the dictation of Lord Shiva from April 22, 2009 "**You are witnessing the genesis of relations of a new type in each sphere of activities on the planet**".

You are witnessing the genesis of relations of a new type in each sphere of activities on the planet

Lord Shiva, April 22, 2009

I AM Shiva! I HAVE come today!

I have come to give a message and I have come in order to assure you that our plans for planet Earth will be fulfilled, in spite of the colossal resistance of the opposing forces!

I have come to strengthen our messenger. I am always there where it is necessary to create a preponderance of forces. I AM Shiva – the destroyer of illusion.

If you want the forces of illusion to leave planet Earth as soon as possible, you should learn a small Teaching on how you should behave now, at this tough time.

We are doing our best, and we expect the same from you.

You notice, and it is impossible not to notice, that the world is changing. And you understand that the process of changing will go on, in the face of resistance of the opposing forces which are scraping the barrel of their resources. The intensity of emotions and the intensity of the conflict are taxing our powers to the utmost.

And in order for you to maintain yourselves as conductors of the Divine energy you should get into the process of transformation.

There is a popular misconception that the whole process of transformation is inevitable and nothing depends on you. There is a popular opinion that nothing should be undertaken in the physical plane, as the physical plane will be ruined and the entire life will transit to a more subtle plane.

Yes, it will be so, but allowing it to happen now will mean that ninety percent of humans are not ready for the continuation of their evolution in the subtle plane due to their attachment to the physical plane of planet Earth.

Therefore, no matter how strongly we want to speed up the process of transformation, we cannot do this out of our compassion for Life. I have come to destroy another illusion in your consciousness. And this is the illusion that you should not do anything now.

Do understand that the establishment of harmony between all the bodies is required. And all your bodies must take part in the process of transformation. In order to develop in yourself the necessary qualities for the transition to the subtle plane it is necessary to develop in yourself an ability to perform any task qualitatively and to direct energy for the process of transformation to proceed as smoothly as possible.

You yourselves can regulate the process of changes on the planet. For this your concentration on the positive, on God, on the Higher plane of existence is required. When you think about the Supreme, follow the instructions of the Ascended Masters and work for the Common Weal – then in this process a new type of relations will germinate which is to replace the old type of relations existing on planet Earth now, but which is to be extirpated.

You are witnessing the genesis of relations of a new type in each sphere of activities on the planet.

You should understand that God can transform the physical plane of planet Earth only with your help, since each of you is a necessary element in the Divine chain. And you will not be able to progress on the path of evolutionary movement without establishing a proper order in the physical plane.

Another way of resolving the situation on the planet is a general global cataclysm in which only ten percent of the population of planet Earth will be survivors, capable of continuing the evolution in the more subtle planes, while, in such a case, the rest will join the waste bin of the universe.

And at this moment each of you decides for yourself which path to follow.

Analyse thoroughly what you are doing during the day and what you are thinking about. In ninety percent of your time you are multiplying the illusion with your thoughts and actions, because you are not directing the Divine energy according to the plan of God for planet Earth.

That is why you should more attentively approach everything that surrounds you and everything that you encounter in your lives.

The illusion is now stronger than ever. And you get an impression that it can never be destroyed.

However, should I just raise my trident, the end to all the illusory manifestation on the planet will come. I am restraining my temper and giving every individual a chance.

The barriers that are slowing down the process of changes on the planet are in your consciousness.

Do not hurry to criticise any man. First look inside yourself and in the lapse of time you will be able to discern. And you will understand that everything that annoys you in your fellowmen is present in yourself, since the illusion surrounding you is the illusion inherent in your consciousness. And when you alter your consciousness your external circumstances start changing.

Now I will reveal a secret to you. You will not die. You will live forever. And the process of the alternation of deaths and births from this moment of time will take place in a different way. You will be born again and remember what you come into embodiment for.

Now we are working in the subtle plane and allow only those souls to be born who agree to act in accordance with the Divine conception. We suspend the embodiment of those souls who resist and do not wish to evolve. By doing this we create more favourable conditions in the physical plane enabling those souls who follow the path of evolution to manifest themselves.

Exactly the same decision was taken in the times of Atlantis. And many souls were not allowed to incarnate. Now the cycles have changed and again favourable conditions for the development of souls must be created on earth.

We are acting very accurately, and we call you for co-operation.

No matter how long your ego resists, it must be pacified. And if you yourselves do not manage to master your beast, we will have to put a straightjacket on it for a time, and times, and half a time.

I AM Shiva!

An important message

The Presence of the One, December 28, 2007

I AM the Presence of the One. I come extremely seldom to the non-ascended humanity.

The sphere of my concerns and the circle of my contacts are far beyond your interests and the intermundane vibrations of your world.

However, I am here. And my coming has been caused by the importance of events...

I come in order to assure you that the Earth, as a planet in general, and her spheres that are close to you will be transferred to the new energetic level. We come in order to prepare your consciousness for this Great Transition.

Do understand that it is enough for just a small percentage of planet Earth's population to get a foretaste of the new ideas and to expand their consciousness to the necessary level, and the whole planet will be flooded by the new thinking and new vibrations. And while before, the process of evolution was taking place gradually, and this gentle process was supported by your earthly Masters, now we have decided to dare to take a leap in the form of a transition to the new energetic level.

Do not be afraid, this leap will not be of a global character and will not lead to the extinction of all the living on the planet.

It would, rather, look like a gentle urge, like the caring pushing of a child towards a new life.

Many of you are still incapable of independent development. Many still hope that all the changes will go past them and they will manage to keep both their old habits and the old state of their consciousness.

However, I have come to destroy this stereotype of your consciousness. Believe me, no matter how you would strive to keep your old comfortable and carefree positions, the time has finally come when it is necessary to break out of the habitual frames and borders.

And as soon as this process of changes occurs, you will tell each other with surprise about how you used to live before with your old level of consciousness. And even when on your physical media you will watch movies and listen to the music characteristic of the present civilisation, you will not believe your ears and eyes – to such an extent the things inherent in the earthly civilisation now will differ from what you are to have in the future.

And this is a natural process. When you are an adolescent, many things seem meaningful and interesting to you. When you mature, you consider your former interests with astonishment.

Everything in this universe is attracted in conformity with the law of correspondence of vibrations. And when your vibrations rise, all your old interests will seem rather strange and absurd to you.

Do believe me and do believe my experience in transferring retarded civilisations to a new energetic level.

I observe with surprise very many phenomena of your civilisation. You have very stark contrasts. And the high vibrations, high patterns in art, music, and painting are intertwined with the low-vibratory and extremely base patterns. Your consciousness is capable of receiving such diverse things. You are able to vibrate in different energetic diapasons.

Well, this only means that it will be easier for you to adapt to the new energetic state. And it will be easier for you to enter the new age of development of your consciousness.

I have come with an amazing feeling of victory in my heart. I anticipate the joy of your souls at releasing from a mass of needless old things and the by-gone junk.

I rejoice at your finally getting free from many habits of the past and that you will be able to become familiar with the harmony of the universe, will be able to join the Oneness of this universe and will be able to be on an equal footing with those civilisations which develop steadily in accordance with the Divine plan.

As you understand, we are forced to interpose in the operation of the law of free will and to curtail your free will a little. But this is a temporary and desperate measure and I hope that the human civilisation of planet Earth as a whole will escape unharmed and will be able to develop reliably and steadily.

I do understand that today's message of mine may cause you a certain anxiety and even be a shock to you.

I don't want you to be frightened or start buying food for future use.

Nothing of what your consciousness can foresee will happen, because all the changes will take place in a very mild way and on those planes of Existence which you have no access to.

You have nothing to fear. We are taking care of you. The whole Hierarchy of reasonable cosmic beings dedicatedly serves many, many civilisations that exist in this universe, including your earthly civilisation.

Our decision was passed by the Karmic Board. The Supreme Council of this universe has yielded consent.

I have given you necessary information today. All the choices you had to make and about which we had been warning you have now been made. Now it remains only to wait for cosmic terms and cosmic opportunities.

I AM the Presence of the One. Om.

All the sense of the prayer-practice is in the raising of your consciousness

Padma Sambhava, April 23, 2005

I AM Padma Sambhava. Do you know me?

I HAVE come through this messenger to tell you something about the task which I carried out during my incarnation on Earth. I came to Earth more than a thousand years ago. I was born by the Mind. I was born in a Lotus flower of the Mind. My level of merit of a Buddha enabled me to come to this world in this way.

Oh, you may not believe me. Many miracles take place on Earth, but if you do not believe in these miracles, they do not exist for you. You believe only in what you see on the screens of your TV-sets and computers.

You believe unreal things to be real, but you are not capable of perceiving the real things.

You will become a Buddha when a reverse process takes place in your consciousness: you will perceive The Divine Reality while staying within the illusion and you will realise all the illusory character of your world.

I HAVE come to Earth to confirm the basis of the belief which was called Buddhism, to renew this belief and to strengthen it. This is my mission. And I am happy to have this opportunity to apply to people who mostly do not belong to the Buddhists.

In reality each of you can become a Buddhist very simply. It is enough for you to come to a decision within your heart not to cause harm to any of the living creatures on Earth, and you are obliged to take upon yourself a responsibility to help all the living creatures on Earth. And if you are ready to fulfil these two promises, you can consider yourself to be a Buddhist from now on.

I have come to you on the eve of Vesak celebration, the full moon in Taurus. I have come to affirm the foundations of Buddhism in your hearts, just as I came with the same mission more than a thousand years ago. Nothing has changed in the world. The world remains in the illusion as before and does not hurry to part with it.

Your prayer-practice should have aspiration. If you pray without proper aspiration, you waste your time in vain. If during your prayer or meditation you are thinking about the greatness of the work you do for mankind, your prayer becomes meaningless.

You should completely leave your human consciousness during your prayer. How can you talk to God, if you have not raised your consciousness up to that level where God will be able to hear you?

When you talk between yourselves you care about coming close to your collocutor so that he can hear you. Why don't you care about the opportunity for God to hear you during your talk to Him?

God talks to you in the language of the heart, and He talks to you within your heart. That is why nothing should refocus your attention during your prayer. You must be completely concentrated on your heart and on the feeling within your heart.

You are not even obliged to utter the words of a prayer at this moment. You simply unite your consciousness with God's consciousness. You raise your consciousness up to the level of your Higher Self. And you are – in God.

The very sense of a prayer-practice is in the raising of your consciousness. If your lips and tongue utter the words of a prayer, but your mind is wandering somewhere around watching people doing their business, you'd better give up your prayer. This is a meaningless occupation for you. A prayer is a communication with God, not an exercise for the tongue. You know that there is a difference in the conception of God in Buddhism. But if your conception of God coincides with the conception of the Highest Law, the Absolute, the Highest Reason, you are sure to become almost a real Buddhist.

It is strange to watch people judging with their human consciousness what God is and what He represents by Himself. And if your personal idea of God does not coincide with the ideas of any other person, you may even feel hostility towards this person. Every man has his own image of God in his consciousness. That is why you should only admit a thought in your consciousness that other people can have different conceptions of God. But this does not mean that some people have a more correct conception, while others have a less correct one.

You become closer to God when you raise your consciousness up to the highest possible level that is accessible for you. The higher the level of your consciousness, the more and more you realise that it is impossible for you to know God. And even when you become god in the eyes of other people, you still will not be able to know God.

There is only an eternal striving to know Being, an eternal surpassing of yourself. But when you reach the state of nirvana in your consciousness, you realise that you have reached everything and you need not know anything any longer because you have entered the state of Divinity.

However, cosmic terms approach and you leave this state and begin knowing God again. And this process has neither beginning nor end.

But now you are at the lowest stage of knowing God and your foremost task is to learn how to differentiate between the illusory world and the Real world. And first of all you have to learn how to differentiate the illusion within your consciousness.

If you scrutinise your thoughts and feelings, you will see that your thoughts and feelings are absolutely unreal. Everything with which your mind comes into contact is an illusion. For that reason, the first stage of liberating yourself from the illusion is your understanding that all your thoughts and feelings represent illusions.

As soon as you realise it, you will be ready for the next step – for the understanding of what is Real in yourselves.

There are many practices of meditation in the world. All of them are aimed at coming into contact with the Real part of yourself. And the first step to your Real part is the soothing of your mind.

I will give you my mantra. I endow this mantra with my energy, with the impetus of my merits. Therefore, if you decide to utter this mantra now, you will receive a maximum effect from the uttering. This mantra will help you give up not only excessive mobility of your mind, it will enable you to get rid of many of your imperfections.

So, you utter with humility:

OM MANI PADME HUM[15]

---

[15] This mantra has been interpreted as "Hail to the jewel in the lotus". The majority of Tibetan Buddhist texts have regarded the translation of the mantra as secondary, focusing instead on the correspondence of the six

Repeat this mantra as many times and as often as you want to do it. This mantra will help you give up your ego as quickly as you can admit it into your mind.

Some people think that they will not be able to give up their ego till the end of their lives. Some people think that they will need a few lives more to get rid of their ego. But only the things which you admit in your consciousness can actually take place. So, if you admit in your consciousness that you will get rid of your ego due to the uttering of my mantra 1000 times a day for a whole year, it will happen.

But, before the uttering of my mantra, don't forget to follow the recommendations which I have given you in this dictation. Don't forget that you are talking to God: do approach Him within your heart as close as possible, so that He can hear you.

I AM Padma Sambhava and I have been with you today on the eve of Vesak celebration.

---

syllables of the mantra to various other groupings of six in the Buddhist tradition. For example: **Om** - Generosity; **Ma** - Ethics; **Ni** - Patience; **Pad** - Diligence; **Me** - Renunciation; **Hum** - Wisdom. (translator's footnote).

Calls from the messages of the summer cycle of 2009 for everyday spiritual practice

"In the name of I AM THAT I AM, I invite my I AM Presence, a divine spark within me, to be with me throughout this day. I ask you, my I AM Presence, to take under your immediate control all my actions, deeds, words, feelings and thoughts. I ask you, my mighty I AM Presence, to act through me throughout this day, to guide my life. Amen."

Master Godfre, July 6, 2009

"Oh, Lord, I am tired of despair; I am tired of unfriendliness and gloomy faces of people. I want transformation! My soul is craving for renewal! My soul is tired and requires new energies to come, the energies of Love, Compassion and Mercy. Help, Lord, and accelerate the process of the transformation of planet Earth!"

Beloved Quan Yin, June 27, 2009

"I know that these states are not real. I know that the illusion is strong, but I am ready to oppose all the power of my Love pouring from my heart against the illusory forces. I love this world. I love God and His creation, and I will not allow this world to be destroyed. Beloved Archangel Michael and the angels of protection, I am asking you to use my lifestream to help the legions of Light. I know that nothing will happen to my planet as long as at least one lightbearer acts consciously on the side of the powers of Light."

Saint Archangel Michael, June 22, 2009

Messages of Ascended Masters

Words of Wisdom - 10

Tatyana N. Mickushina

Translated from Russian by
Svetlana Nekrasova and
Ekaterina Reznichenko

Editor: Svetlana Nekrasova

Proofreader: Alison Lobel

Websites:
http://sirius-eng.net (English version)
http://sirius-ru.net (Russian version)

20924014R00065

Made in the USA
Middletown, DE
12 June 2015